W. C. Titcomb

475 Palmer Ave

SUIT OF LIGHTS

The Author.

SUIT OF LIGHTS

By

VINCENT CHARLES HITCHCOCK

FREDERICK MULLER LTD
LONDON

791.82
H674s

FIRST PUBLISHED BY FREDERICK MULLER LTD
MADE AND PRINTED IN GREAT BRITAIN BY
WILLIAM CLOWES AND SONS, LIMITED
LONDON AND BECCLES

CONTENTS

		page
Chapter	1	9
	2	22
	3	40
	4	50
	5	68
	6	84
	7	103
	8	120
	9	140
	10	162
	11	186
Glossary		205

5

DEDICATION

I dedicate this book firstly to the memory of my father, by whose patient forbearance I was allowed to achieve my desire to become a *torero*, and secondly to my wife, without whose help and encouragement this book would never have been written.

LIST OF ILLUSTRATIONS

The Author   *Frontispiece*

Facing page

Jose Moya, Castillito, the author, Vicente Escribano, Minuto and Enrique Vera in Linares bullring   32

The first *derechazo* I made   32

Leaving for my first fight with Miguel Ropero and Pedro   33

Waiting to start the *paseo* at my debut between Miguel Campos and Pepe Chapi   33

Pronouncing the dedication of my first bull   64

The end of the fight; being carried shoulder high   64

A *veronica*   65

A *natural*   65

A *derechazo*, with a fast-moving bull   96

Terminating a *faena* with a *pase de pecho*   96

A two-handed *pase por alto*, following through   97

A right-handed *pase por alto*   97

Lining up to make the kill   128

The *estocada* is completed and the sword is home   128

A *manoletina*   129

A narrow escape   160

The author with Juan Belmonte   160

Leaving Algeciras bullring with ears and tail   161

Talking to an *aficionado* before presentation in Madrid   161

A *media veronica* in Madrid, and its consequences   192

Taking a heavy toss in the Madrid bullring   193

With the ears of the last bull I killed in La Linea   193

7

LIST OF ILLUSTRATIONS

The Author . . . . Frontispiece

                                                   facing page

Left: Myself, Ortillo ..., my mother, Vienna Barahona, blanca and Lentpue Vas 'a time in ball ...   25

The first drawing I know ...   27

Learning to ... my first fight with Miguel Ropno and Pato ...   29

Waiting to start the pause at my debut between Miguel Gaspar and Pepe Campo ...   31

Pronouncing the dedication of my first bull ...   64

The end of the fight: being carried shoulder high ...   64

A veronica ...   65

A natural ...   65

A derechazo with a fast-moving bull ...   96

Terminating a pass with a pase de pecho ...   96

A two-handed pase por alto, following through ...   97

A right-handed pase por alto ...   97

Lining up to make the kill ...   127

The estocade is completed and the sword is home ...   128

A superman ...   129

A veronica passes ...   160

Two passes with Juan Belmonte ...   160

Leaving Madrid after brilliant with cape and tail ...   161

With the team of novices before presentation in Madrid ...   161

A single estocade in Madrid and its consequences ...   192

Taking a heavy toss in the Madrid bullring ...   192

Within the gates of the hospital I lingered in La Linea ...   193

1

"*AHORA! Ahora!*" shouted a man seated a few rows below where my companion and I were sitting in the *Plaza Monumental de Madrid*, the most important bullring in the world. I turned to my friend Ricardo, a young Mexican medical student whom I had met on the train from Paris. "What is he shouting?" I asked. "He is a *valiente* of the seats, one of those fellows who have never faced a bull, but like to sit up here and tell the *toreros* how they should fight. He is telling the *matador* that now is the time to kill the bull; of course he is wrong—they usually are, these armchair critics —it is impossible to kill a bull when it is in its *querencia* like this one."

I had learned from various books on the subject of bullfighting that when a bull forms a *querencia*, that is, when it decides to stay in one particular part of the ring for which it develops a preference, the bullfighter is obliged to lure the animal away to some other part of the ring before attempting to pass or kill it. The bull inside its *querencia* is on the defensive rather than the attack, and consequently will wait for the man to come to it and then will hook out and gore.

Evidently there were many *valientes* amongst the spectators at this fight, for cries of "*Ahora!*" ("Now!") were coming from all over the tiers of seats. The *matador* was young and rather inexperienced and this was his presentation fight in Madrid, an ordeal in itself. Already one *matador*, two *banderilleros* and a *picador* had entered the bullring operating theatre for various wounds, two of them quite serious.

9

The young *matador* looked bewildered. He had made several attempts to draw the bull away from the fence where it had taken up its *querencia*, but the animal would advance a step or two and then return to its original position.

"I think that he is going to attempt to kill it where it is," my companion informed me. "It is sheer madness. He will join his companions in the *enfermeria*, you see. It will be chloroform, not wine, for that one tonight."

My hands started to sweat as I watched the boy line the bull up and go into the kill.

Now there were cries of "No! No!" from the public. Hell, I thought, they don't know what they do want. My mind flashed back to Vicente Blasco Ibanez's attack on the bullring public in his book "Blood and Sand".

The young *matador* was sighting along the blade of his sword, his weight on his right leg and his left leg slightly bent, the red lure held low in his left hand and across his body. They say that the left hand kills more than the right, because it is the left hand that, by managing the cloth and making the bull drop its head, enables the *matador* to go in over the horns and place the sword between the beast's shoulder blades.

The bull stood still and tranquil, watching the bullfighter's every move. Crossing his left hand over his chest to lead the bull past, the *torero* went in over the horns, but just as my companion had predicted, the bull hooked out, and we saw and almost heard the horn rip into the boy's groin. The bull lifted its head to toss. As soon as the *torero's* feet were off the ground, his own weight spun him on the horns like a badly made tinsel-covered propeller. The bull tossed and the *matador* hurtled through the air to crash in the sand some twelve feet away. He lay on his back in the sand, inert and very exposed. We could see the blood pumping through the hole in his groin, his life blood going out with every heart beat. "The femoral artery," said my companion, "*muy grave*, very grave indeed."

Immediately the bull had gored, the other bullfighters had started out from the barrier to draw it away from their fallen companion so as to get him to the operating table as soon as possible. They had obviously anticipated such a situation. Fast as they were, the bull was faster. It wheeled and came at the boy again. It was lively enough now. Its confidence was restored; it had hit something solid and spilt blood. It arrived at the motionless body before the bullfighters and was trampling and goring again. Eventually it was drawn off. The injured *matador* was lifted off the ground and rushed to the barrier, where the attendants were waiting to carry him to the *enfermeria*.

They passed him over the barrier just below where we were sitting, and to our horror we realised that when the bull had gored him again while he lay on the ground, the horn had ripped open his belly and now his guts lay exposed whilst the blood still pumped from his groin. One of the attendants tried to plug the hole with his thumb in an attempt to staunch the flow of blood.

The whole thing had taken only seconds, but I felt as if I had been sitting there for hours watching this grisly incident. There were no *valientes* shouting now. There was silence. The fight was over and people were leaving. There was no buzz of conversation, no animated discussions between the fans. Just silence.

My companion led the way from the bullring to a bar across the road. He ordered two brandies. Neither of us spoke. We downed our drinks and ordered two more. After a few minutes my companion broke the silence.

"Well?" he said.

I said nothing.

"Do you still want to become a *torero*?" he continued.

"Er, yes, of course," I replied; "I can't go back to London now, not without even making an attempt."

I felt sick and very scared. We had some more brandy.

"Look, Vicente, this is not for you, this business of the bulls. It is supremely dangerous."

"I knew that before I came. I had read Hemingway."

"But you told me yourself that you thought Hemingway had exaggerated the danger involved and coloured bullfighting generally."

"I'm still not going back to London. Apart from having to face my family and friends and admit defeat, I know I shall never be satisfied until I have experienced it out there in the ring alone with a bull."

By now the brandy was taking effect and my confidence was returning.

"All right, my *amigo*; it is your life, not mine. Maybe one day you will become a *maestro* and dedicate a bull to me in Mexico City. By that time I shall have qualified and will be able to sew you up myself."

"Let's go," I said. "I want to see if I can get a ticket for the Andalucia Express for tonight. Then I shall be in Algeciras tomorrow—and then to the real business of learning to fight bulls."

I had previously decided to go to Algeciras and then to Gibraltar, so that I might learn Spanish and get myself a job whilst I learned to become a *matador*. It was all going to be so easy.

We took a taxi to the station of Atocha. Arriving at the station, my companion told me to wait while he found out when I could get a ticket. After a while he returned. "I have managed to get you a sleeping berth for tomorrow night. It will cost you an extra 300 pesetas, but it is the only thing available," he told me.

"All right," I conceded. "I'm anxious to get down to Gibraltar. I have already spent far too much money here in Madrid."

We went into the station together and purchased the ticket.

12

"As this is your last night in Madrid we will go to a show—at my invitation," suggested Ricardo. "Gloria Romero is singing. You will enjoy it. All *tipico* stuff—you know, *flamenco* and dancing with castanets; but first we will go down to the *calle de la Victoria*, where we bought the tickets for the bullfight this morning, and we'll have some wine. I want to find out how that *torero* is, although it is almost a certainty that he will be dead by now. If Dr. Jimenez Guinea—the bullring surgeon in Madrid and the finest horn wound specialist in Spain—has managed to save him, it will be a miracle. Nothing short of a miracle. The human body just isn't built to withstand that sort of treatment."

In the bars in the *calle de la Victoria* everyone was talking about the goring of that afternoon. The worst seen in Madrid for many a year, some said. Everyone had a different version of the outcome. Some said that the boy had died before reaching the operating table. Others said that he had been operated on, but had died in the ambulance on the way to the bullfighters' sanatorium. Still others said that Dr. Jimenez Guinea was still operating. All agreed that if the boy was not already dead, he certainly would not live long.

Suddenly there was a commotion outside. "Stay here," said Ricardo, "and I will see what it is all about." After a few minutes he returned.

"It was one of the male nurses from the infirmary, and he says that the boy has been operated on, but is in too bad a condition to be moved to the sanatorium. They have called in the priest." My companion made the sign of the Cross.

"Let us have some more wine," I said. I did not wish to talk about the accident any more. My doubts were beginning to return once again. "You were going to take me to a bar that specialises in *criadillas*," I told Ricardo. *Criadillas* I knew to be the bull's testicles, which when fried and eaten with a light dry wine are considered a delicacy.

13

"Come on then," said Ricardo, and proceeded to lead the way through the labyrinthine passages that abound in that quarter of Madrid.

Eventually he halted before the open door of a bar which, like most of the bars around there, was adorned with faded bullfight posters and hung with stuffed heads of bulls whose varnished horns glistened in the harsh electric light and whose lifeless glass eyes surveyed the swarming humans drinking at the bar with disdain and superiority.

The *criadillas* were served. My companion proffered me the dish and, not without some apprehension, I forked a piece and ate it. It was delicious.

"Do you like them?" enquired Ricardo.

"They are delicious," I replied.

"Therein lies the courage and *noblesse* of the bull, the great god Taurus. Eat, eat all you can, and perhaps you will acquire a little of these qualities," said Ricardo.

My friend was getting a little drunk, as indeed was I.

It was now nearly ten-thirty and the theatre started at eleven. I suggested that we should take a taxi as I was anxious not to miss any of the show.

Like most shows of its kind in Spain, it consisted of a star who was very good, a couple of supporting stars who were fair and a chorus that was lousy. The idea of a chorus dancing as a team just doesn't exist in Spain. Each member dances as an individual and has one aim in life, that is to attract attention to himself or herself and to distract attention from the rest of the chorus. The culmination was a lament for Manolete, who had perished in the bullring at Linares exactly a year previously.

I had read accounts of the death of Manolete—who has been described as the *matador* of the century—in the British press and quite a lengthy profile of the *maestro* in an American magazine. From these I had gathered that he had been something extraordinary, and that his death had made a great impression all over the world. I did not, however, expect to see men in the audience crying openly as the singer sang a lament before an image of the *matador*, illuminated with a single spotlight, in a theatre in Madrid a year after his demise.

All this helped to strengthen my resolution to find out more about bullfighting and to experience the sensations involved in being in mortal combat with a wild beast alone in the ring and before thousands of pairs of critical eyes.

I went to bed in a very pensive mood that night and did not manage to fall asleep until nearly dawn.

Spaniards are notoriously late risers, but when I came down for breakfast the hotel was deserted.

"Could I have some coffee?" I enquired.

"Coffee? But this is the time for the *aperitivo, señor*. Would you like some vermouth or wine?"

Vermouth for breakfast! I acquiesced. My Spanish was not strong enough for me to be able to protest. Indeed, apart from *si* and *no* I was lost. I said *si*.

"With or without soda, *señor*?"

Hell, what was the difference, it was still a devil of a breakfast.

"Without soda, please."

I drank my breakfast and went out.

I had to find out whether the trunk containing all my clothing had arrived from the French frontier, so I went down to the *Estacion del Norte* to make enquiries. I could not make anybody understand me. Eventually an interpreter, whose English was about half a dozen words better than my Spanish, came to my rescue. We hunted high and low, but there was no trace of my trunk. I gave the fellow a couple of pounds and the number of the baggage ticket; he promised to find the trunk and forward it to me at Algeciras.

After eating a late lunch I went out to meet Ricardo, who was coming to the station with me to see me off.

15

We arrived in plenty of time and installed my grip—my one and only remaining piece of luggage—in the sleeping compartment, which I noticed I should have to share. I had visions of spending the night trying to carry on a conversation in sign language with whoever was to be my *compagnon de voyage*.

Ricardo and I descended to the platform to make our farewells.

The engine, a huge and ponderous affair, seemed to be groaning and ready to burst at every seam. The fires glowed red, and the driver and fireman, their faces hot and shining, laboured like the devil's assistants to get up even more steam. The whistle blew. We were en-route for Algeciras. And then?

I made my way back to my sleeper. A dark-haired man was seated on the lower bunk. I guessed that he was my travelling companion. We exchanged a salutatory "*Buenas noches*".

The train by this time had gathered speed and was rocking and roaring along the track. Foot by foot we were passing another rocking and roaring monster. We swayed from side to side as one does on those torturous devices one pays for the privilege of riding on at fairgrounds.

I looked at my companion. He smiled in return.

"*Que vamos a ganar!*" he said.

I looked blank and replied, "*Yo, ingles.*"

"Ah! You are English? I speak a little English. You speak Espanish?"

"No."

"Do not be worried by the train. This happens every night. You see, the Andalucia Express and the Catalan Express leave the station at the same time and always there is a race to see who first reaches the points where the tracks separate. Tonight, I think we win."

I looked out of our window. Our engine was leading by some twenty yards. Just at that moment, our driver gave one long and then several short blasts on the whistle. The other driver replied, and then we rattled over the points and the Catalan Express swung over and off to the left. Our driver continued shrilling on the whistle.

"The cock wins and now he crows," said my companion.

"Isn't it all rather dangerous?" I asked him, remembering how they had stoked up.

"Nothing has ever happened so far, so why should it now?" This, I was to find later, is a Spanish philosophy which is applied to most things.

"You have been long in Spain?"

"No, only a few days."

"You will stay a long time here?"

"I am going to Gibraltar."

"For your holidays, perhaps?"

"No, to work."

"And your work is?"

"I was in the diamond business in London with my father, but I will do other work when I get to Gibraltar. I do not know yet what I shall do."

"I know Gibraltar. Very good whisky. Cigarettes. My brother lives in La Linea just across the frontier, you know. I used to live there too. I learn English there but now I do not speak English. I forget."

"It is very good. I shall be very happy if I learn Spanish half as well as you know English."

My companion looked very pleased at this.

I did not feel that I should tell him about my desire to become a bullfighter.

"Shall we go to dinner?" he asked.

"Yes," I assented.

We made our way to the dining car. I told my companion to order for me. The meal was no better than its counterpart on British Railways, its one redeeming feature being the

17

abundance of good cheap wine. We both took advantage of this.

We returned to our sleeper as dusk was falling, the warm red glow of the setting sun softening the harsh lines of this rugged plateau of Castille.

I picked up and started to read my copy of Hemingway's "Death in the Afternoon", but found that I could not concentrate on reading so I turned to the pictures. My companion, noticing that I was looking at photographs of bullfighting, asked me if I was keen on the *corrida*—as the bullfight is known in Spanish.

"You like the *corrida*?" he asked.

"I am very interested," I replied. "I have read all I could find written in English about it."

I decided to confess to my aspirations.

"I would like to become a bullfighter," I said.

"You! An Englishman a *torero*?" ejaculated my friend. "That is impossible. One must have Latin blood to be able to appreciate and feel about things like our *fiesta nacional*."

"There have been foreign bullfighters," I replied.

"Yes, Portuguese, Mexicans and South Americans and even one or two Frenchmen, but an Englishman! Impossible. You have not the *temperamento*."

"There was an American. From Brooklyn, I believe," I continued.

"But he lived in Mexico and acquired the feeling through environment," said the Spaniard.

"Then I shall do the same here," I replied.

"How do you propose to start?" queried my friend. "You don't even speak Espanish. Are you going to start a new fashion and speak to the bulls in English? The bullbreeders will not like that. Not only will they have to breed fierce bulls but also teach them English," he said laughingly.

This, I thought, is what I shall have to put up with all along

18

the line. Nobody is going to take me seriously. The idea of an Englishman wishing to become a bullfighter will be considered ridiculous. I could see that I would be the butt of many jokes. My most difficult job would be to assure the Spaniards that I was serious about it all.

"Tell me," I asked my companion, "isn't bullfighting an art?"

"The greatest, the most beautiful and the most difficult in the world," he replied.

"And tell me," I continued, "isn't art international? Isn't it said that art knows no frontiers?"

"True. I admit that, my friend. Maybe if you had been born here or if you had lived here for many years it would be possible. Do you realise that most bullfighters start training at the age of ten or eleven and that many of them actually fight young animals out on the ranches before they reach the age of thirteen? Also, they have talked and heard talk of bullfighting for the whole of their lives. They are, you might say, born with a cape in their hands. But you, I suppose you are twenty-one or twenty-two?"

"Nearly twenty-one," I confessed.

"Well, how do you expect to do in a few months something that takes boys born to the life years to achieve?"

"I shall do my best to remedy this," I said.

"I wish you luck, *amigo*. I wish you plenty of luck. How do you propose to train? Do you know any bullfighters or bullbreeders? It is very important that you should get to know the breeders. It is when they hold their *tientas*, the try-outs when the cows are tested for their bravery to determine whether they are fierce enough to be used for breeding fighting bulls, that the bullfighters have a chance to practise with live animals."

"Unfortunately I know nobody in Spain; that is why I am making for Gibraltar. While I learn Spanish there I hope to be able to make contact with the bullfighting fraternity in La Linea. I must first find myself a job in Gibraltar and then cross the border whenever possible. Maybe I shall find someone there who will give me lessons."

"I will give you a card to my brother who owns a printing works in La Linea," offered my friend. "He prints the posters and leaflets for the bullfights there and consequently knows the management of the local bullring."

I thanked my companion for his offer. At last some progress was being made. I looked forward to the future with more confidence.

The train continued shrieking and rattling its way towards the South. My companion was already asleep in his bunk, and soon afterwards I also dozed off.

The sound of the water sellers shouting "*Agua, agua fresca*" and the thumping of luggage being shifted woke me with a start. I sat up in my bunk and saw that my friend was preparing to leave. He turned to me and seeing that I was awake said, "This is Ronda. I leave you here. You are now in the country of the bulls." He offered me his hand. "*Adios, torero.* I hope to see you again and that you will be a *matador* by then. Don't forget, as soon as you arrive in La Linea you must go to see my brother. Rest assured that he will do all in his power to help you. I shall be telephoning him later and I will tell him to expect you. *Adios* and good luck."

I watched through the open window as my friend picked his way between groups of people who apparently had nothing better to do than watch the arrival and departure of the train. The time was 3 a.m. and the station was crowded. Groups of soldiers stood around being jostled by the pedlars—pedlars of water, pedlars of bread, pedlars of lemonade. A woman was walking the length of the train offering a live but obviously very startled hen for sale. It seemed that it was possible to buy anything at this station in the early hours of the morning.

I have never failed to wonder at the curious assortment of people that turn out in the middle of the night and throng even the tiniest and remotest stations throughout Spain. No matter what time it is, there are always multitudes of nondescript persons loafing on the platforms.

After a halt of nearly twenty minutes, the train resumed its journey southwards.

Leaving Ronda, the track follows a steep downward gradient between the towering peaks of the *sierra* and nearly doubles back on itself in a wide and steep curve.

One side of the track was lined with fig trees, their large, hand-like leaves shimmering gently in the cool night breeze that blew down from the mountains. Mountains that stood like huge silver sentinels, their peaks bathed in moonlight so brilliant that they appeared to be capped with snow.

Down by the stream running along the other side of the track the bullfrogs were croaking a *basso profundo* accompaniment to the tenors and altos of the cicadas and crickets. The night was filled with the music of the wild.

At a distance a camp-fire blazed, and I could imagine a group of gipsies encamped there. Probably—if they were not asleep—one of them would be singing a *fandanguillo* or a *seguidilla* to a rhythmic handclapped accompaniment.

This was Andalucia; the very air was exciting and the blood seemed to race in my veins as I thought what the morrow might bring.

For an hour or more I sat at the window and watched the moonlit panorama that flashed before my eyes. I was tired, very tired, but so afraid that I might miss something that eventually I had to force myself back to my bunk and to the sleep that was needed to make me fresh and alert for tomorrow's encounters.

2

I AWOKE early and, after washing and shaving, made my way towards the dining car for coffee. I walked to the rear of the train but found the dining car to be missing. After consulting my English-Spanish dictionary I asked one of the attendants where I could obtain a cup of coffee and something to eat. To my horror he told me that the dining car had been taken off at Bobadilla, a station up the line, whilst I had slept. He offered me a drink from his wine skin, showing me how to hold it at eye-level and shoot a jet of wine into my mouth. I soaked my face and shirt-front but managed to direct some of it down my throat, and, although my stomach protested violently, I felt somewhat refreshed.

We were passing through the cork forests of Almoraima, and these shortly gave way to open scrub-covered range where herds of grazing bulls moved off at a gentle trot at the approach of the train. They looked so docile and gentle out here on free range that I could not identify them with the fierce and noble beasts of the bullring.

The train passed through mile after mile of bull country and eventually drew into a tiny station. From the notice board I gathered that this was San Roque and the alighting stop for La Linea. I was debating whether to detrain here and go to La Linea first, or travel on to Algeciras and take the ferry across to Gibraltar, when the train began to move, so I had no choice but to continue the journey to Algeciras. I am glad now that I did, because later I discovered that the so-called station of La

Linea is some six to seven miles away from the township and the only means of transport is an ancient taxi.

Soon we arrived at the terminus and the train drew right into the dockside. The business of passing through the Customs was soon accomplished, and in no time I found myself on the ferry nosing its way across the bay to Gibraltar.

Approached from this direction the Rock makes an attractive picture, and seeing it again conjured up memories of my last visit.

I was serving at sea as Deputy Purser on the s.s. *Madura*, a steamer belonging to the British India Line. One evening when we were about three days out of Liverpool I went to my bunk feeling pretty sick. The sea was calm, so I knew that it was not seasickness; indeed, I had never been troubled in that way and I had been in some pretty tough seas. The next morning the doctor came to my cabin and diagnosed appendicitis. The ship was put about, I was taken ashore in a tender and in a matter of half an hour I was being operated on.

The operation was completely successful, but my recovery was very slow and I had to spend some three weeks or more in bed. Eventually, however, I was allowed to get up and go for short walks in the afternoons.

One of the nurses in the hospital told me that it was possible to obtain a permit to visit Spain, so I applied at the Spanish Consulate and was given a carnet allowing three trips across the border. As I was to be discharged from hospital the following Sunday morning, I decided to use the first on a visit to La Linea and watch the bullfight that was billed for that afternoon.

Bullfighting was completely unknown to me and I was expecting to see nothing more than a blood bath. I had always imagined it to be a modern taurobolium. However, I found that the blood did not perturb me unduly as the bulls at no time appeared to be conscious of the wounds inflicted upon

23

them. The pageantry and ritual appealed to me but the actual fighting left me cold. I left the bullring remaining unimpressed and unenthusiastic.

It had been the topic of conversation for some days that the much-vaunted annual fair of Algeciras was to begin on the coming Thursday, and everyone in my hotel insisted that I should see it. I decided to go and managed to persuade Bill Allen, purser of an American ship, and fellow bar-crawler, to accompany me. He spoke a little Spanish, and I thought that this would be a great asset.

We took the ferry to Algeciras, and immediately on arrival there could sense the excitement and gaiety in the air. We made our way to the fairground and did a tour of the side-shows, taking glasses of wine at the booths that tempted us with various wines and ice-cold beers enticingly displayed. Suddenly my American friend informed me that he intended going to the bullfight, and I, rather than be left alone, decided to go with him.

The bullring in Algeciras was somewhat smaller than the ring in La Linea, and there was no double barrier between the spectators and the arena. We had good seats right in the front row, almost on top of the bulls; in fact we were so close that I was able to lean over the barrier and pluck a dart from the shoulders of a bull as it stood below where we sat.

The experience of having already seen one bullfight the previous week enabled me to watch the proceedings without being distracted by the pageantry, and therefore to be better able to appreciate the work of the bullfighters, who were not so proficient as the three I had seen at the other fight. Now the danger was more obvious, and I was forced to change my ideas about the stupid bull always following the cloth and never going for the man.

One man was tossed and carried out of the ring, another *matador* taking his place. I turned to my companion.

24

"I should have thought that that bull's life would be spared now that it has caught the bullfighter," I said.

"Yeah, the poor sonofabitch don't stand a chance," Bill replied.

At that moment a man sitting behind us butted in.

"Excuse me, this is first time you see a bullfight?"

I informed him that I had seen my first fight in La Linea a week previously and that this was my second experience.

"It is very difficult for non-Latins to understand," the man, who turned out to be a Gibraltarian, told us. "You see, the bull is not supposed to stand a chance. Bullfighting is not a sport. It is not a contest between the man and the bull. The bull always is killed, that is the destiny of all bulls all over the world. The bulls that do not die in the bullring die in the slaughterhouse. No, bullfighting is an art, a pure art. It is, you might say, a ritualistic killing of bulls. The man may be killed executing his art, but if he is, his death is incidental. The important thing is the beauty created by the man with the beast and the climax of the man killing the animal."

"The cruelty is unnecessary," I admonished.

"But life is cruel, very cruel. The bull is a killer, it is bred for that. Remember, nothing is done to provoke the bull to fight, it is let loose in the ring and attacks of its own free will. I am convinced that if the bull had to choose between dying in the ring and dying in the slaughterhouse it would choose to die in the ring. A bull shows no fear in the ring—but in the slaughterhouse! Have you ever been to a slaughterhouse?"

I admitted that I had, in England. I remembered the beasts I had seen there, eyes wide with fright, awaiting their turn to die. Awaiting their turn to be roped and dragged across the blood-and-intestine-strewn floor of the slaughterhouse, to be brought ignobly to their knees. I remembered, too, how I had seen the slaughterhouse men break the tails of the animals to make them move when they tried to resist being dragged to their death.

25

"Fear is far worse than pain," our enlightener continued. "Imagine yourself in a concentration camp and being given the choice of dying in the gas chamber or taking on their champion in a duel to the death. Which would you choose?"

"To fight for it of course," I replied.

"Naturally. When the bull comes into the ring it does not know that it does not stand a chance, that it has to die anyway. The wounds it receives during the course of the fight, are they not received in hot blood? You will admit that such wounds are usually not painful at the time of their being inflicted. It is afterwards when one is calm and the numbness wears off and the nerves start functioning again that the pain really starts. The bull is dead before it has time to think about its wounds," he concluded.

As we watched the last bull of the afternoon fought and killed our outlook changed. We rose to leave, and at this our friend behind invited us to go with him for some wine. For the rest of that evening we talked of nothing but bulls and bullfighters. My interest was growing.

"You will come to watch the fights tomorrow?" asked the Gibraltarian.

"I am afraid that I am due to sail at dawn," said Bill, whose interest in bulls lay mainly in the steaks they provided.

"I should like to come again," I said quickly.

"Then why not come with me? I have not bought my ticket yet. We will get two seats together and you will be able to appreciate the things I have been telling you tonight."

We made our way back to Gibraltar. I was clutching my precious dart which my newly found friend, who introduced himself as Señor Perez, informed me was called a *banderilla*.

After arranging a rendezvous for the next day I bade him good night and, wishing Bill *bon voyage* and good hunting, made my way back to my hotel to bed. I was looking forward to the morrow.

Señor Perez and I took our places in the bullring early, and from the time the first bull entered the ring until the carcase of the last bull was dragged out he explained every detail to me, pointing out particular passes and situations of which he had spoken the previous night. I came away from the ring vowing to learn all I could about bullfighting and, if possible, to come back to Spain one day. This was to be my last visit here for some time, as I was due to leave for India the next day.

By the time we left the ring Señor Perez was Paco to me and I was Vincent to him, and as it was essential to seal our friendship with wine we went down to the fair. All the excitement, gaiety and wine soon got the better of me and it was not long before I was merry. Later that night, on returning to the hotel, I was told that my company's agent had been looking for me as I was to join the *Orontes* as a passenger to Bombay.

Next morning, with a head full of memories and thick from wine, I sailed for India.

By now the ferryboat was pulling into the quay by the Customs sheds at Gibraltar.

I disembarked and went through the Customs formalities and then through the Immigration Office. Here I was informed that a resident's permit was necessary if I wished to stay on the Rock. I was given a permit allowing me to stay overnight, and I promised to report to the police station in the morning.

Before leaving England some friends had given me the address of their son who was serving as a captain with the R.A.S.C. in the garrison. I sought out his house and rang the front-door bell. The door was answered by an attractive Spanish maid.

"Is Captain Graham at home?" I enquired.

"*Si, señor, espera usted un momento.* I call the Capitan."

I waited, and in a few minutes a good-looking, suntanned, but obviously English, man approached.

"I am Vincent Hitchcock," I began.

"Come in, Vincent. I'm Johnny Graham. My parents wrote to me and said that I could expect a call from a mad character who wants to eat bulls alive."

"Thanks," I said, following him into the house.

"Seriously, old man, do you really want to become a bull-fighter?"

"Yes, I do; although how I'm going to do it I don't quite know. Nobody seems to be very optimistic so far."

"I know several Gibraltarians who are great fans of the bullfights and I'll introduce you to some of them. But first you must have a shower to freshen you after your long journey," my host offered.

He led the way upstairs to the bathroom.

"There you are. If there's anything you need, just shout."

The shower was more than welcome. The stinging hot water stimulated me in body and mind, but I cursed my luck for having lost my trunk and consequently not having a change of clothes.

Bathed and refreshed, I descended the stairs to the living-room, where my benefactor introduced me to his wife, a charming person who, as it turned out, shared his enthusiasm for the bullfights and who, like myself, had not been terribly impressed by her first fight but later, understanding more about it, had become a devotee. We drank and talked about my prospects.

"You will need somewhere to live, of course. I would love to offer you a room here, but, as you see, space is limited and we have two children and a maid living in," said Johnny's wife.

"Please don't bother," I said. "I shall find some cheap digs somewhere."

"It isn't easy, you know," Johnny informed me. "The Rock is very overcrowded and accommodation is scarce. However, we may be able to find you a room at the Methodist Mission—but we can start worrying about that after dinner."

True to his word, after a very good meal Johnny took me down to the Methodist Mission and I was lucky enough to get a very pleasant room for £1 per week.

We met again the next day and he came with me to the police station to apply for a resident's permit. The officer-in-charge said that I could have a temporary one provided that I found a job, but it was rescindable in the event of my not being able to do so. He advised me to try the Labour Exchange.

Thanking Johnny for his help, I made my way to the Labour Exchange.

"Ever been in the building trade?" the clerk asked me.

"No, but I would like to try it," I replied.

"There are some big blocks of flats being built here and they need labourers. The wages are very poor, but you will have to accept the local rates. Here is a chit for the general foreman."

I took the note and went along to the building site and asked for the foreman.

"Can you paint?" he asked.

"Oh, yes," I lied.

"Right, start in the morning 7.30 a.m. sharp. Two pounds ten a week, half-day Saturdays, no overtime. You can eat all your meals in the canteen if you wish."

I thanked him and made my way back to my room.

Next morning at 7.30 a.m. sharp I reported for work. Having no clothes other than those I stood up in, I reported to the painting foreman wearing a lounge suit, collar and tie. He looked at me aghast and said:

"Who do you think you are, a bloody gaffer?" I felt embarrassed and mumbled that I hadn't any other clothes. He,

29

being a warm-hearted fellow, offered to lend me a pair of overalls which I gladly donned.

All day I toiled at sandpapering wooden window and door frames, and by the time five o'clock came I was worn out and finger-sore. Tired as I was, I hurried home to clean up, as I wanted to cross the border into La Linea and find the printer who, I hoped, would start me on my career as a *matador*.

Finding the printing works was a simple job and I enquired if the proprietor, Señor Vallejo, was there. The man I was talking to informed me that he was Señor Vallejo and asked who I might be. I showed him the visiting card his brother had given me on the train. He read it quickly and then said, smiling:

"I have been expecting you. My brother telephoned me from Ronda the other day and told me about you and your wish to become a *torero*." I found this Señor Vallejo to be as amiable as his brother.

"I am closing the works now," he said. "If you care to wait a minute, we will go and find Adolfo Beaty. He is the British Pro-Consul and also, in conjunction with his father, impresario of the bullring here. If anyone can help you, it is Adolfo."

I waited, and when he was sure that everything was securely locked up he bade me follow him. After enquiring at the Consulate where we could find Beaty, we knocked at the door of his flat, which was in the same building. Señor Vallejo introduced me and left me with the Pro-Consul.

"Whatever gave you the idea of wanting to fight bulls?" enquired Beaty.

I told him of the time I had been landed in Gibraltar and the bullfights I had seen.

"And you decided there and then that you wished to become a *torero*?"

"Oh, no; I rejoined my ship in India and served for another

two years until my demobilisation number came up. Meanwhile I read everything that I could lay my hands on that dealt with Spain and bullfighting," I replied.

"And then?" encouraged Beaty.

"I returned to England and worked for my father in his business in Hatton Garden, but I was bored to tears and the urge to go abroad again grew stronger every day. Slowly the idea of becoming the first Englishman to be a bullfighter matured," I continued.

"What made you finally decide to come out here and risk your life?"

"It is rather strange. There was a company of Spanish dancers in London; they were the first Spanish dancers to perform there since the war and they created quite a stir. I saw every performance except the matinées, and one evening I met a young Spaniard who also had seen nearly every show. We became friends and I told him that I had this idea of becoming a bullfighter. Subsequently we met each evening prior to the show, and one night after an exceptionally rousing performance he took me round to the dressing rooms to introduce me to Carmen Amaya, who was the star of the company, and after the introductions told her that I had some crazy idea about becoming a *torero*. I felt awkward and expected Carmen to laugh but instead she looked at me with her deep-seeing gipsy eyes and said: 'Yes, you go to Spain. You will become a *torero*.'

"And turning to my friend Jose, she said: '*Tiene cara de torero*. He has the type, he will fight the bulls, you will see.'

"I decided there and then that I would come to Spain. The next day I bought my ticket and applied at the Spanish Consulate in London for a transit permit to travel overland through Spain. That was two weeks ago—and here I am."

"Do you mean to say that you packed your bags and came out here on the advice of a gipsy dancer?" asked Beaty incredulously.

"I didn't need much encouragement. In fact hers was the only encouragement that I received."

"You have a very difficult road ahead if you are determined to carry out your plans. First, you must learn how to use the cape and *muleta*. This you can do here in La Linea if you wish. You must go to the bullring every day and practise with the other local boys who are trying to become *toreros*. I warn you that it is extremely difficult, even for Spaniards. You must learn how to 'shadow bullfight', then learn the theory of bullfighting, and when you are competent you will have to put your theory into practice. Believe me it is quite an experience when you stand before a bull for the first time. Even the smallest of bulls looks like a cathedral when you are in front of it armed only with a cape."

"Can you introduce me to these young lads?" I asked.

"Certainly, I'll do that this evening," he promised.

"But I have no cape yet," I told him.

"Never mind, the other boys will let you use theirs until you can buy one of your own. Come with me now and we will go down to the *Circulo Mercantil*—that is a sort of business man's club here where I meet my friends every evening. We discuss nothing but bulls."

We went down the main street of La Linea towards a large building in front of which the pavement was lined with wicker chairs mostly all occupied. On seeing us approach, a group of men greeted Beaty who motioned me to sit down. I made for one of the chairs.

"*Hombre, por Dios*," said Beaty, "don't sit there. That is reserved for El Mosquito. Don't you see it is bent out of shape? That is the only chair that El Mosquito fits into."

Looking at the chair I noticed it was indeed misshapen, the seat being depressed and the arms splayed.

Beaty, or Adolfo as he insisted I call him, introduced me to the company and told them that I was to be the new taurine

32

In Linares bullring Jose Moya points out to Castillito and myself the spot where Manolete received his fatal goring. The
other bullfighters are Vicente Escribano, Minuto and Enrique
Vera. (*Below*) The very first *derechazo* I made at my first *tienta*
on the ranch of Don Juan Gallardo. (*Photo: Perez-Ponce.*)

(*Above*) Leaving for my first fight. In the car with me is Miguel
Ropero, my manager, and behind him in an open-necked shirt
Pedro, my swordhandler. (*Below*) Waiting to start the *paseo*
at my debut between Miguel Campos and Pepe Chapi.
(*Photos: Perez-Ponce.*)

wonder. I couldn't help noticing the ill-concealed smiles that greeted this statement.

"You must come to my studio and have your photograph taken in a bullfighter's clothes," said one chap whom I afterwards knew as Jose Perez Ponce, an excellent photographer and specialist in action shots of bullfights.

I nodded noncommittally, as I felt he was mocking me.

Presently a huge man approached. I was quite right in surmising that he was the Mosquito. He grunted something and lowered himself into the protesting wicker chair.

"Don Jose," said Adolfo indicating El Mosquito, "owns the local slaughterhouse and also buys the meat of the bulls killed in the bullring here. When you have practised a little maybe he can arrange for you to fight a small bull."

Adolfo turned to El Mosquito and repeated in Spanish what he had just told me in English.

"You come to slaughterhouse tomorrow eleven o'clock," he told me.

I must have looked startled because the others began to grin derisively. I turned to Adolfo.

"Does he expect me to fight a bull?"

"Don't worry, they are only kidding you, but you must appear eager and be there at eleven o'clock. They won't really put you in front of a bull, but turn up, otherwise it will be all around the town that you are scared," Adolfo assured me.

I was uneasy, but knew that I had no alternative but to appear at the slaughterhouse next day. Apart from anything else it meant taking the morning off from work and losing half a day's pay. I went to bed that night a very apprehensive aspirant bullfighter with doubts crowding my mind. Supposing they did loose a real bull on me? By the time I fell asleep I had died a hundred ignominious deaths on the horns of a bull.

Next morning I arose early, and after breakfast made my way across the border into La Linea and to the slaughterhouse.

On arriving there I was dismayed to find quite a crowd present and evidently waiting for me. I was introduced to a young boy, Miguel Campos, who, I was told, was to make his professional debut in La Linea in a few weeks' time. Miguel, beckoning me to follow, led the way through the slaughter-house to the corrals at the back. The first corral was deserted; crossing this I followed Miguel through a narrow slit in the stone wall opposite. Inside the second corral was a herd of bulls and bullocks. On hearing us enter, one of the largest bulls with huge low sweeping horns turned and stared at us.

"That is the one we will cape," said Miguel, indicating the enormous beast.

"But," I began, and then quickly swallowed my words. At all costs I was determined to show no fear, although I was beginning to feel rather sick. What chance had I against a bull when I did not even know how to hold a fighting cape?

I turned to Miguel. "I do not know how to hold a cape, let alone make any passes," I said, half hoping that this would excuse me from performing.

"I will show you," said Miguel, "I have an old *muleta* here that you can use."

We went back into the empty corral and Miguel produced his rather faded *muleta* and a stick which was to represent the sword. He then proceeded to show me how to spread the cloth of the *muleta* with the stick and hold both in my right hand.

"That's right," said Miguel. "Now I will show you the statuesque passes. Put your feet together like this, hold the *muleta* out in front of you and stand in profile to the bull."

I took the *muleta* and stick from Miguel and copied what he had done.

"Fine, fine," he encouraged. "When the bull looks at you, shake the *muleta* gently to fix its attention, and when it charges just stand perfectly still and wait until the horns are

34

almost touching the cloth, then move the *muleta* in the direction the bull is charging and lead it past you."

It sounded easy and with Miguel acting as bull I tried a couple of passes. There was a burst of applause from the direction of the slaughterhouse door. Several people had congregated there and were watching the proceedings. The head slaughterman came forward.

"That's good," he said. "Now try it with a bull."

He walked over to the door dividing the corrals and swung it open. Miguel motioned me to stand behind one of the little wooden barriers that were placed around the walls of the corral at intervals. They resembled the little safety barriers used in the bullrings, which are just wide enough for a man to slide behind, but too narrow to admit a bull.

There was shouting coming from the next corral and then, with a clatter of hooves, through the door trotted the large bull. Immediately the door closed behind it. The animal trotted completely round the corral and stopped some twelve feet away from our plank shelter.

"Now," said Miguel.

I ran out towards the bull and spread the cloth of the *muleta* in front of me and stood straight, with feet together, about six feet from the horns of the beast. I shook the *muleta* gently and watched the bull's eyes move from me to the lure. "*Aha, toro!*" I shouted. The bull just stood and looked. I moved a foot nearer and repeated the process. Still the bull just gazed fixedly at the *muleta*. Again another foot nearer. "*Aha, toro!*" I cried, and then I stamped my foot as I had seen the bullfighters do.

Instead of charging, to my astonishment the bull turned tail and fled. There were shouts of laughter from the spectators. I couldn't figure out what had happened and then Miguel came out to me. He was smiling.

"I am sorry, Vicente, we have been pulling your leg. That

35

was a meat animal and not at all dangerous. He would have run from his own shadow. But you did very well all the same. Nobody expected that you would attempt to face him."

Although I was rather annoyed that I had been through all the worry and uneasiness for nothing, I was somewhat cheered when Miguel told me that I had created a good impression.

"They are going to shut in a one-year-old calf for me in a minute," said Miguel. "If you would like to try those passes I'll let you have a go with him."

Eagerly I accepted and followed him behind the shelter again while the calf was let into the corral. This time the animal tore into the corral like a whirlwind and then pulled up in the centre. I could see the tossing muscle in his neck rippling in anticipation. Miguel slipped out from between the planks, and immediately the young bull wheeled and came straight at him. Pushing the *muleta* out in front of him Miguel caught the bull's charge and with a long sweep of his arm guided the animal past him.

After executing several series of passes Miguel called to me: "Take him now, Vicente."

I stepped out and Miguel handed me the *muleta* and stick. "Do exactly as you did before," he advised.

I approached the bull slowly and then without warning he came charging straight for me. I pushed the *muleta* out towards him and then felt the side of the animal brush against me as he tore past. The next thing I knew was that he had turned and come for me again. I was taken unawares and before I could react I was lying on my back and the bull was trampling on me. Miguel rushed out and with his body as a lure, led the bull away from me. Several pairs of willing hands helped me to my feet.

Having disposed of the bull, Miguel approached me.

"That was not too bad," he said. "At least you stood still and had control over your feet. That's half the battle."

The congratulations of those who had witnessed my first

encounter with a bull exhilarated me and made me forget my bruises for a while, and I left the slaughterhouse feeling like a conquering hero. I had actually been in front of a bull, even if it was only a very little one!

Miguel accompanied me to the frontier.

"If you would like to come over to the bullring every evening at seven-thirty you can practise with me," he offered.

I said that I would be delighted to, and promised to be there the following evening.

The next two weeks were really hard going, working all day and practising every evening in the bullring. Miguel advised me to learn first how to make the *veronica*, which is the pass with the cape on which all other passes are based. Hour after hour I swung the heavy fighting cape until my arms ached, but with the encouragement of Miguel and the other lads who used the bullring for the evening practice sessions, I was gradually able to execute a fairly presentable *veronica*.

The day of Miguel's debut grew near and each evening when we met I could sense him becoming more tense. He had invited me to watch him dress for the ring and when at last the great day arrived I felt as if it were I, and not Miguel, who was to enter the ring that afternoon.

Miguel had taken a room in an hotel as he did not wish to upset his mother with the performance of dressing and leaving for the ring from his home.

The process and ritual attached to the "dressing" intrigued me and once again I was reminded of the fact that I had a tremendous amount to learn about bullfighting apart from the ringcraft. Whilst he was drawing on his pink stockings—an essential part of a *matador's* clothing—I picked up Miguel's *montera*, the black flat-topped hat that bullfighters wear in the ring, in order to see how I looked in one. I tried it on and then made as if to place it on the bed, when Miguel's sword handler fairly jumped on me. "*Dios mio*, do you wish us bad luck?"

he shouted. I must have looked blank for he continued: "Do you not know that it is bad luck to put any hat on a bed? Especially that of a *torero*! And just when he is about to leave for the *plaza*!"

The fight went off very well and Miguel made an extremely good job of both bulls. He was on the first rung of the ladder of success.

That evening a group of friends and I were discussing the fight over a glass of wine in the "Bodega Jerezana", a bar in La Linea, when one of the company, a haulage contractor named Ramon Frutuoso, asked whether I would like to ride on the lorry with him the next day when he had to return the spare bull to the ranch of Don Juan Gallardo who breeds bulls just outside Algeciras. I jumped at the opportunity as I had not yet seen a ranch, and also Ramon promised to introduce me to the bull-breeder. We arranged that I should be at Ramon's house early next morning.

Although it meant taking another day off from work I was at the house dead on time. Two or three of the other lads I had met in the bullring were there to lend a hand and after loading the bull on to the lorry we set out for Algeciras.

The ranch-house and corrals nestled in the foothills north of the town and in every direction stretched wide open range. In the distance we could see herds of bulls like black dots on the horizon.

After making enquiries we discovered that Don Juan Gallardo was not at home, so Ramon decided to loose the bull into the practice ring that is a part of every ranch where fighting bulls are bred. Not without difficulty the bull, a large black beast, was freed and stood snorting at us as we sat atop the high wall enclosing the ring.

One of the young would-be *toreros* with us suggested that we should try a few passes using a jacket as a cape, but Ramon would not hear of it.

"Don't you realise that bulls must never be fought before they enter the ring?" he said. The boys murmured that of course they knew this, so nothing more was said and we set off back to La Linea.

Ramon dropped us off at the bullring as we had decided to have a practice session. After entering the ring one of the lads whom I knew as El Niño called us together. "Listen, who is willing to come out to the ranch tonight to see if the bull is still in the ring? It is almost full moon and it will be light enough for us to try our luck with the cape." Two of the lads readily agreed but the others dissented. "What about you?" they asked me. Without thinking I agreed to go along with them. "You will have to stay over here all night. What about your pass?"

"I know the frontier guards well enough now to risk it. I am sure they won't mind," I assured them.

The fighting of bulls at night-time by young aspirant *matadores* is quite common in Spain and I had read in Juan Belmonte's autobiography how the young boys go out and fight the bulls in the open country. A highly dangerous practice on account of the bulls and also the *Guardia Civil* who shoot on sight anyone interfering with the animals.

The thought of the danger excited me and I waited restlessly for the hour to arrive when we should set out. Of necessity we had to go on foot, and owing to the distance to be travelled and the nature of the country to be crossed, we were to leave fairly early.

Eventually my impatience got the better of me and I went to the arranged rendezvous half-an-hour before time. Presently two of the boys arrived; the one who had suggested the escapade and the other who had promised to bring an army groundsheet which was to serve as a cape. We waited for nearly an hour for the fourth boy to appear and then came to the conclusion that he had backed out, so we set off by ourselves.

3

WE followed the road from La Linea to Algeciras as far as Campamento. Here it was decided that we should cut across country in order to avoid the *Guardia Civil*, who patrol the coast road with thoroughness as a precaution against the smugglers who are very prevalent in this area. Climbing steadily, we skirted the village of San Roque where the *Guardia Civil* have a barracks and also a road block where all traffic from La Linea is stopped and, if necessary, searched.

By now the moon was well up and its light enabled us to see our way without too much difficulty, but it also helped the *Guardia Civil*, who have a reputation for keen eyesight and sharpshooting.

The excitement was, to me, like a tonic. I thrived on the danger. It reminded me of my schooldays when we used to break bounds in the middle of the night to go poaching or raiding neighbouring chicken-houses. This time, however, I was very aware that death might be close at hand.

The country over which we were passing was rough and rock-strewn, dotted here and there with clumps of prickly-pear cactus, a form of vegetation to be well avoided. The cactus plants threw eerie shadows and Manolo, the boy who carried the groundsheet, peered fearfully at each one as if he imagined the whole of the *Guardia Civil* were out that night, disguised as cacti.

A terrified rabbit bolting from almost under our feet made us start with fright. The three of us were beginning to get jumpy, but nobody wanted to be the first to suggest that we should turn back, so on we trudged.

Crossing a narrow lane I saw five long, otter-like creatures cross our path. They ran with their backs arched like stoats and each with its nose almost touching the tail of the one in front. They were about the size of large otters and, as they ran, emitted a peculiar, high-pitched chittering sound. I later found out that they were grey mongooses and were of the species that abound in Africa.

"What are they?" I enquired of my companions.

"They are called *meloncillos*. They hunt rabbits and stink to high heaven."

Indeed I had caught a strong whiff of musk as they had passed us. Obviously they were not animals to have around the house.

By now we were topping a hill on the boundary of the Gallardo ranch and were able to see a cluster of white buildings in the distance. On and on we plodded. Soon we could plainly distinguish the outline of the practice ring. The brilliance of the moonlight gave the white walls of the ring and adjoining corrals an ominous cemetery-like appearance. Now our hearts were really beating wildly.

Stealthily approaching the ring, we walked round it until we found the flight of stone steps leading to the top of the wall at a point where the corrals joined the ring proper. Hurriedly we scrambled to the top, each one anxious to be the first to see if the bull was still there.

The ring was nearly half in shadow and at first we could not see the bull, but could plainly hear him as he scrambled to his feet to face the intruders who dared disturb his rest. There he stood, regal and beautiful, the moonlight enhancing the splendid sheen of his coat. His black-tipped horns shone like silver poniards as he shook his head, daring us to take a step nearer. We walked along the top of the wall until we were above the plank shelter which stood eighteen inches away from the wall of the ring.

"Vicente, you and I will go in here, and you, Manolo, take the other shelter," our ringleader instructed.

Manolo ran lightly round the top of the wall and dropped silently behind the planking. The bull watched this manœuvre with interest, and whilst his attention was distracted El Niño and I dropped behind our shelter.

"I'll take him first," said my shelter mate. "Give me the cape."

I handed him the groundsheet which Manolo had put in my care. It then struck me that if any of us got into a tight corner or was tossed, we had no second cape with which to draw the bull away.

I was alone in my cramped hiding-place. I looked out over the top of the planking and watched my companion stand calmly before the bull with the cape outstretched before him. The bull was taken aback by the effrontery of this creature that had dared trespass on his domain and as El Niño stepped forward whispering "*Aha toro, mira bonito*" the animal shot towards him as if projected from a catapult. El Niño stood his ground, and with a forward and downward sweep of his hands guided the bull past him in a graceful *veronica*. "*Olé!*" from Manolo and myself simultaneously and "*Olé!*" a second time as El Niño followed through and brought the bull past again in the perfect style of the Sevillian school. Legs slightly apart, feet firmly planted, hands held low and body pivoting from the waist. Here was the *veronica* at its best.

El Niño was one of those unfortunate individuals who could never perform his art in public. On several occasions he had been given fights but always, through sheer stage fright, had made a complete mess of things; and this was the boy who could do such things with a bull as I was witnessing. He executed several more passes and then finished with a half *veronica* winding the beast tightly around himself.

"Here, Manolo, you take him now," said El Niño as he handed over the cape. "I'd give him a minute or two to get his wind back," he advised.

Manolo waited a moment before stepping out to the bull. I had guessed from watching him during practice sessions that he was one of the showy and rather vulgar type of bull-fighter who always seemed to be trying to commit suicide on the bull's horns. I was rather apprehensive of what he would attempt now.

The bull had turned his attention to Manolo as soon as the latter had left the plank shelter, and was now watching his every move. Manolo ran out with short jerky steps, calling to the bull as he did so, and then, as the bull started for him, dropped to one knee and swung the cape over his shoulder and behind his back. The bull's horns missed his head by inches.

Manolo now stood erect, but still with the cape behind him. He was obviously going to attempt some *gaoneras*—a pass where the body is exposed to the bull as the cape is held behind the back, rather like a *veronica* in reverse. This is not particularly dangerous when executed in daylight but at night-time this pass, in which movement is greatly restricted, is supremely dangerous. Manolo appeared oblivious of the existing perils and stepped up to the bull.

My heart was in my mouth as I watched the bull charge again but Manolo made the pass unscathed. The animal wheeled and came again, so close this time that its shoulders brushed Manolo, throwing him off balance. Almost before he had touched the ground, El Niño was out from the barrier luring the bull away from the fallen figure. It was a very risky operation but one obviously done without thought for personal safety. His only concern was for a comrade in danger. I later came to find that this was the general rule amongst bull-fighters. Whatever jealousy exists among them is purely professional and never personal. I have seen bullfighters and bullring attendants take unbelievable chances to save a fallen comrade.

Manolo, seeing his friend's action, immediately leapt to his feet and in the nick of time turned the bull's attention from El Niño as the latter made for the plank shelter where I was still crouching. The incident had happened so quickly that I hadn't thought of what I should do.

As El Niño slid in beside me, I apologised.

"I'm sorry I didn't help, but you were out there before I realised what had happened," I said.

"Don't worry, Vicente. We are always prepared for situations like that one and we practise what to do until it becomes a reflex. You will find that when you have a little more experience you will do the same."

Then came the awesome question. "Do you want to try now?"

Of course I wanted to, although I was scared stiff after what had just happened.

"Manolo, let Vicente have the cape," called El Niño in a low voice.

Manolo walked backwards away from the bull over to the shelter where I was wishing I could remain. He handed me the cape.

"Let's see those *veronicas* now," he said, "and good luck."

I took the cape from his hands and feeling too frightened to reply, stepped out towards where the bull was standing in the shadows. Spreading the cape before me I advanced step by step, my feet felt leaden, and I wanted to relieve my bladder, but it was too late now; the bull was only a few feet away.

The moonlight glistening on its back and on the curve of its horns made it look twice as large and several times more

44

deadly. I shook the cape and called it but as the beast started for me I took fright and, throwing the cape over the advancing horns, turned and ran, the bull hard on my heels. I slipped behind the shelter just as the horns splintered the planks behind me.

El Niño caught me in his arms, otherwise I would have probably collapsed. "You must get the cape back again," he said. "Manolo and I will distract the bull while you get it."

I was petrified at the idea but realised that I had no alternative. Manolo and El Niño picked up pieces of dried bull dung and began throwing them at the beast while I slipped out from between the planks. The cape lay on the ground some twenty feet away. To me it seemed more like a hundred yards. Almost on tiptoe I stole up to it and then, bending my knees so that I would not have to take my eyes from the bull for one instant, I picked it up.

With the cape in my hands once again I was filled with the realisation of my action. I had run away in the face of my adversary. The next day all La Linea would know that the "Englishman Who Wanted To Become a Bullfighter" was a coward. Determined to redeem my reputation I gripped the cape and faced the bull again. "*Aha toro, aha,*" I called and shook the cape. He came at me and I swung the folds of the cape out and down past me as I had practised. Before I could think, the bull had passed and was facing me again. I repeated this three or four times and then cut his charge short with a *media veronica*; this is a half-pass which is designed to turn the animal sharply on to himself and to allow the bullfighter to walk away.

My companions were applauding; I had made it. I turned to the bull and did a few more passes, then El Niño called to me to finish. It was getting late and we had a long walk ahead of us.

We left the ranch feeling exhilarated and congratulating ourselves on having followed in the footsteps of the great Belmonte. I did not realise at the time the selfishness of our actions or the damage we could have done. A bull having once been caped becomes impossible to fight, and instead of following the lures will go for the man. Even if a bull is caped at the age of a few months and not fought again until years later, it will remember its previous experience and will soon figure out that the man and the cape are separate objects, and that the cape is inanimate and only a tool in its adversary's hands. It is always stated in the bullfighter's contract that the bulls he is to kill are virgin. That is why once a bull enters the ring, even if the bullfighter cannot kill it, it must be slaughtered. There are exceptional cases where the life of the bull is spared but these are very few and far between, and in such cases every precaution is taken to ensure that the bull will not be used again. Usually the points of the horns are sawn off and the animal is used for stud.

In Portugal, where the killing of the bulls in public is prohibited by law, the act of entering for the kill is simulated and a *banderilla* is placed in the spot on the bull's shoulders where the sword should have entered. The bull is then led away from the ring and slaughtered.

I do not know why this law is in being, whether it is supposed to be less cruel or whether it is supposed not to offend the sensitive Portuguese. In my view it is very cruel indeed as it enables the animal to calm down and feel the agony of its wounds and to realise that it is being led away to die.

The feeling of confidence, born of our successful exploit, made us decide to return to La Linea by road. It was about 5 a.m. and the sun was well up and softening the hard contours of the countryside that had seemed so very severe and terrifying the previous night.

As the road rose steadily to San Roque we could look out over the shimmering silver blue water of the bay. Manolo began to sing a flamenco song, an *alegria*:

> "*En lo alto de la sierra*
> *Cordoba tiene un cortijo,*
> *Donde le dio Largartijo,*
> *Las primeras lecciones a Guerra.*"

El Niño accompanied him by beating out the rhythm with his hands and snapping fingers. I attempted to follow, but the broken tempo was a little beyond me. I determined that this was another thing I had to learn.

It was nearly six-thirty by the time we reached La Línea, and we were all feeling very tired. We went to the market and had coffee in an early morning café that catered for the market workers. Manolo and El Niño said that they were ready for bed, as indeed was I. The thought of the day's work that lay ahead of me was distasteful, to say the least of it.

Crossing the border without any difficulty I went straight to the building site and started work. I was put on sandpapering cupboards and doors, a tedious job in any circumstances and by the afternoon I was ready to drop. Then a wonderful idea occurred to me.

The cupboards I was working on were divided into two parts with a long door at the bottom and a smaller door above, and as yet the dividing boards had not been put in. I decided that if I could wedge the bottom door from the outside and then climb in through the top, I would be able to take a nap in peace. I did this but my respite was short-lived. The next thing I knew was that I was sitting half-asleep on the floor of the cupboard and the foreman was standing over me raving and fuming. Needless to say, from then onwards I was an ex-painter's mate.

The situation was now desperate. I could not renew my

47

Card of Residence without work to do, and I was without a job and with very little prospect of finding one.

I consulted Adolfo Beaty and he suggested that I should apply for a permit to live in Spain so that I could spend more time training. My only worry was how I was to live in Spain. I had no money at all, I could speak very little Spanish and there was absolutely no possibility of my finding a job inside Spain. Regardless of this fact, I decided to apply for a visa.

After having the necessary photographs taken and with the requisite guarantees from two persons resident in Spain, I applied at the Spanish Consulate in Gibraltar for a temporary resident's visa. I was presented with a huge form full of the most intimate and seemingly unnecessary questions. One of the questions read: "Why do you wish to reside in Spain?" I filled it in stating that it was my ambition to become a *torero*. The consulate clerk, on seeing this reply, looked somewhat startled.

"You wish to be a bullfighter, *señor*?" he asked.

"Yes," I replied.

"You have seen a bullfight, *señor*?" he continued.

"Yes," I said again.

"Tell me, *señor*, have you ever seen a bullfighter caught by the bull?"

"Yes, I have," I replied, now a little impatient.

"*Caramba!* And still you wish to fight bulls?"

I said that in spite of this it was still my intention at least to try to become a *torero*.

The clerk smiled, obviously thinking that I could not be quite normal mentally. "We will have to give a visa in that case," he said.

Within three days I had my visa.

Adolfo Beaty, who was my guiding star and adviser at this period, suggested that I should raise some money somehow and make for Madrid, adding that he would give me letters of introduction to people there who would help me. This was a fine idea, the only drawback being that I hadn't the faintest idea as to how I could possibly raise the money for the fare.

It was after I had left Beaty in La Linea and returned to Gibraltar that the solution occurred to me. Walking along Main Street I suddenly noticed a familiar sign—three brass balls! Some minutes later I returned to the pawnbroker's with every pawnable thing I had, my trumpet, a gramophone and a silver cigarette-case. The owner of the pawnshop was very generous and allowed me almost the value of these articles, and also stated that I need not worry if I could not redeem them within the year as he would hold them for me until I returned.

With the money in my pocket and feeling more confident as a result, I packed my bag, bade farewell to my friends in Gibraltar and crossed into La Linea. As I could not afford to spend the night there I was forced to book a ticket on the afternoon train for Madrid.

Adolfo Beaty came to see me off and hand me the letters of introduction that he had prepared and also a cordoban sombrero which he said I was to wear on arrival in Madrid. He insisted that it would make me conspicuous and therefore easily recognisable by a friend of his, a bullfighters' manager named Apolinar Garcia Martin who was to meet me at the station. I did not relish the idea but Adolfo was adamant. He said that the *Madrileños* would be tickled pink by it. I agreed to risk it.

Soon the train pulled out and once again I was en-route for Madrid.

4

ALTHOUGH somewhat apprehensive of the turn events might take in Madrid, I was looking forward to being back in that beautiful city. The little I had seen of it during my brief stay there had endeared both the city and its inhabitants to me; the *ambiente* appealed greatly. It strikes the happy medium between the bustle of Barcelona and the indolence of Sevilla. There is a constant air of gaiety which is more purposeful than that to be found in the south of Spain.

The other passengers in my compartment began to reach down their luggage from the racks and I gathered that we were nearing the end of our journey. Following Adolfo Beaty's instructions, I removed my tie and left my white shirt buttoned at the neck, after the fashion of the bullfighters, and looking in the mirror on the wall of the compartment I adjusted the silver-grey sombrero on my head, pulling it slightly down over the right eye. Two or three of the passengers gave me curious glances and I began to wish that I had never agreed to the idea of wearing the thing, but it was too late now. Obviously Beaty's friend Apolinar would be looking for someone tieless and sporting a conspicuous Andalucian hat.

The platforms of the station were thronged with the usual mass of people so I decided to wait until the crowd had thinned and then stand on the steps of the carriage in order that I might easily be seen. I waited five minutes, ten minutes, a quarter of an hour; by this time the platform was almost deserted, apart from a few porters and railway guards. I was furious, having had to wait so long and feeling so terribly uncomfortable and all to no avail. There was nothing left for me to do but to take the *Metro* to the city centre and find Apolinar's house.

By the time I reached the station of Callao which I knew to be near the address I was seeking, depression weighed heavy upon me. I began to appreciate the feelings of a foreigner in a strange place. Suspicious of everything and everybody, I was certain that people around me were talking about me and having a good laugh at my expense. I was pushed and jostled in the train and the conviction that I was being taken advantage of because I was so obviously a foreigner grew within me. Looking back now, I realise that the Spaniards must have taken me for a compatriot for they are exceedingly courteous towards foreigners and, apart from the odd black sheep, never take advantage of them.

Following the directions of a patient and kindly traffic policeman I soon located the building in which Apolinar's flat was situated and after consulting the concierge climbed to the second floor, where I found a door bearing a brass plate on which was engraved in bold lettering the information "Apolinar Garcia Martin, *Asuntos Taurinos*". It is customary in Spain for people to have their trades or professions stated on their visiting cards. Letters are always addressed in the same way. In this case the plate stated that Apolinar's business was "to do with bullfighting" which, like the term "Import-Export", can cover a multitude of sins.

I rang the door bell and presently the door was opened by a dapper, grey-haired man with a rather English-looking face. He looked surprised to see me and enquired if I was the Englishman from Adolfo Beaty. I affirmed that I was, and Apolinar quite calmly replied that he was just ready to leave for the station.

"But the train arrived over half an hour ago," I expostulated. "I waited at the station for you for a quarter of an hour."

"I am so sorry," said Apolinar apologetically, "but I overslept this morning. The important thing is that you have arrived all right. Where are you going to stay in Madrid?"

I told him that some friends of mine in La Linea had given me the address of a cheap *pension*—a small family hotel—and showed him the address.

"Come along then, let us go there first and get you settled; then we will go and have some wine somewhere. I will introduce you to a few of the Madrid bullfighting circle. By the way, I would leave that hat off; they are not worn here."

We took a taxi to the Plaza de Santa Barbara and found the *pension La Vizcaina*. A portly blonde woman opened the door to us and I gave her the card that my friends had given me. After introducing herself as Margarita and telling us that she was the owner of the *pension*, she bade us follow her. She showed me a small room overlooking the *patio*.

"You can have this room for twenty-five pesetas a day, full board," Margarita offered.

Twenty-five pesetas a day was a little under five shillings and much cheaper than I had dared hope. I gave my new landlady a month's rent in advance. It left me precious little for any other expenses, but the gesture obviously pleased Margarita. She beamed and assured me that she would look after me as if I were her own son.

After unpacking my bag and washing, I followed Apolinar down to the *Puerta del Sol* which is Madrid's equivalent of Piccadilly Circus. Starting from the *Calle de la Victoria* which I already knew, Apolinar led me from one bar to another, introducing me to a great number of people as we went. Some were *picadores*, some were *banderilleros* and some were *matadores* —all were either directly connected with bullfighting or fans of the fiesta. It seemed to me that Apolinar knew just about everybody in Madrid.

That afternoon I lunched at Apolinar's flat and we spent

the rest of the day discussing bullfighting and plans for my future. My host suggested that I needed a manager and that he was quite willing to look after my affairs if I so wished. I decided that it would be a good idea and asked him to draft a contract.

The next day, accompanied by my prospective manager, I went to the big Madrid bullring where he introduced me to several young bullfighters who were practising there. They were all very friendly fellows and promised to help me to learn the intricacies of their art.

During the following week I worked hard, practising both with the cape and the *muleta*. My Spanish still left much to be desired and I found that I learned most by just watching the other fellows in their workouts and then trying to copy them and allowing them to correct my faults. It was slow going but little by little I was picking it up.

At the end of the week Apolinar telephoned my *pension* and said that he had the contract prepared if I would care to meet him and peruse it. . . . We arranged to meet in a bar owned by a *matador* named Gitanillo de Triana whose place, which is called *La Pañoleta* after a small private bullring in Sevilla, is much frequented by *toreros*.

Apolinar gave me the contract to read, but I had great difficulty in getting the gist of it so I decided to send a copy of it to Adolfo Beaty and ask his advice. Apolinar watched me carefully as I scanned its contents.

"I think I had better take it home with me to read it carefully at leisure as there is much that I do not understand," I said.

"As you wish, Vicente, but believe me, it is quite fair," my manager answered.

"Of course," I agreed, "but you must admit that it is necessary that I understand all the conditions."

Apolinar agreed that I should take a copy of the contract

53

home with me so as to read and understand it thoroughly. This would give me an opportunity to send it to La Linea for Adolfo Beaty's approval.

That afternoon I went to the Main Post Office of Madrid, a palatial building in the *Plaza de Cibeles*, and posted the contract express delivery to Adolfo. I did not have to wait long for an answer; the next evening I received a telephone call from La Linea. Adolfo was very excited. On no condition was I to sign the contract as it was impossibly severe and it meant that Apolinar would have almost complete control of my life for the next five years and apart from having to pay all expenses I would have to pay him ten per cent of all moneys I earned, whether from bullfighting or any other sources. I thanked Adolfo for his help and assured him that I would not do anything without consulting him first.

When I told Apolinar what I had done he was surprisingly indifferent about it and did not appear to be in the least concerned. He did in fact offer to introduce me to a friend of his who would look after my interests. The friend in question turned out to be a little man, an *ex-banderillero* named Manuel Castillo, known professionally as Castillito, who had long since been forced to retire from the ring owing to several serious gorings.

Castillito and I became good friends, and he handled my affairs for me although we agreed not to sign a contract until after I had made my professional debut. He accompanied me to the bullring every morning for training and obtained permission for me to visit the Municipal Slaughterhouse each day so that I might learn the art of the *descabello*. This is the method by which a bull is killed if, after the swordthrust is made between the animal's shoulder blades, it does not drop almost immediately. A sword somewhat shorter than the thrusting sword is employed. The object is for the *matador* to lower the bull's head and sever the spinal cord between the back of the skull and the first vertebra. It is a spot in line with the back of the beast's ears and dead in the centre of its neck. *Matadores* often spoil a good performance by not being able to administer this *coup de grâce* with the first stab.

A small cross-piece is attached to the blade of the *descabello* sword about six inches from the point; this is in case the bull should throw its head and send the sword up into the public. Spectators have been killed that way.

Each morning the maid would call me at 5.45 a.m. and with a borrowed *descabello* sword I would go to the slaughter-house. The butchers were very co-operative and gave me plenty of opportunity for practice. Some days I would kill as many as seventy head of cattle and became proficient enough to get a hundred per cent average.

One day I had killed some twenty or more beasts when a large bull was brought in. A rope was thrown round its horns and the other end of the rope passed through a steel ring set in the floor so that the animal's head might be lowered. I stood in front of the beast with my sword ready to administer the death blow, my right knee almost touching the animal's muzzle, when unexpectedly the bull hooked at me with its horns. I jumped back to avert an accident but unfortunately I had not noticed that I was standing in front of the blood sump. I went in, up to my thighs in blood. Going home in the overcrowded tram I had all the room I wanted and everybody stared at me wonderingly. Dangling a sword, and gory as I was, I must have presented a somewhat grim spectacle. Every time I moved, a black cloud of flies buzzed up from my trousers.

The training was progressing very satisfactorily, but I was worried financially, so I wrote to my father and asked whether he could send me some money. It was a seemingly endless ten days that I had to wait for his reply. He said that he was sending £40 to Gibraltar for me, and it was up to me to pick it up and find means of getting it into Spain. I made arrangements for a friend of mine in Gibraltar to collect the money and send it up to Madrid. Meanwhile, I was absolutely penniless.

Castillito was always hard up as he had a wife to support and only a very small pension from the Sevillian Bullfighters' Benevolent Fund to live on. The only other person I knew in Madrid who might lend me a few shillings was an Englishman who was Reuter's correspondent there. I telephoned him and asked him if he could lend me twenty-five pesetas (about five shillings) so that I could buy some cigarettes and one or two odds and ends I needed. To my amazement he refused, saying that he himself was hard up! I resolved there and then that in future I would not ask help from any of my fellow countrymen.

I was trying to decide whether to approach the Conde de Villapadierna, whom I had first met in La Linea and again in Madrid, when the maid came to my room and told me that there was a man asking for me. It turned out that he had my money for me. The first thing I did was to rush out and buy a packet of cigarettes—it was four days since I last had one. Hurriedly I lit up and drew the smoke down into my lungs, and momentarily blacked out!

The next month or so was really hard. I had to budget very carefully and watch every penny. To make matters worse the weather was beginning to turn cold and I had no coat. Up till now I had thought of Madrid as being perpetually bathed in sunshine, but how mistaken I was! Although it had been hot during the summer it was now extremely cold.

The one bright spot during this period was the arrival in Madrid of a Tom Arnold ice show. It was the first of its kind in Spain. Very quickly I made friends with the girls from the show, and we spent many enjoyable times together. If it hadn't been for their kindness I would have spent a very lonely twenty-first birthday. As it was they gave me a pleasantly unexpected party.

As Christmas approached the days grew colder and colder and I found that I was the only one down at the bullring in the mornings. I still did not possess a cape or *muleta* and as there was nobody there to lend me one I practised using my jacket as a cape.

The cold weather made my thoughts turn again to my lost trunk in which I had several pullovers and some warmer suits. I asked Castillito to help me locate it and in vain we pestered the officials of the Spanish Railways. They cabled every station from the frontier to Madrid and from Madrid to Algeciras, but there was no news of my baggage. Then Castillito thought of an idea. Maybe it had been mislaid on the way from Paris to the frontier.

Together we hunted out a Frenchman whom Castillito knew, who was a great bullfight fan. This gaunt-looking character with a beak-like nose accompanied me to the offices of the French Railways. To my delight the clerk in charge not only found my trunk, but showed me a sheaf of correspondence from his office in Paris dealing with their efforts to trace me.

Finding my trunk and at last having a change of clothes to wear gave my morale such a boost as a woman experiences wearing the latest Paris creation. I was further encouraged by a letter from my father saying that he was sending me another £40 for Christmas.

I looked forward to Christmas with some excitement. I would now be able to afford a few luxuries and join in the festivities. The ice show girls were organising a dinner with the usual turkey and trimmings and a party at their hotel afterwards. I had felt embarrassed about accepting their invitation as I wouldn't be able to afford any presents, but now everything would be all right after all.

Days passed and Christmas grew nearer but still there was no sign of my money arriving. I spent the days wandering amongst the stalls that had been set up in the sidestreets of old Madrid. Stalls bearing all the merchandise associated with Christmastide; gaily coloured gifts of glass and bright metal and stalls of decorations and toy trumpets and tambourines. I noticed that some stalls were covered with artificial faeces which looked remarkably authentic. The man who made them must have made a life-long study of such things.

Christmas Day arrived and still there was no sign of my money. The dinner was excellent, the turkey perfect and the wines superior. After the dinner I went with the ice-show girls back to their hotel for the party and on entering the room where it was to be held, the first thing that I noticed was a huge Christmas tree laden with presents. Silently I wished that I could turn tail and flee, but it was too late. Never have I felt so mean. Every one of the girls had bought me a present and I had been unable to give them anything in return.

It was not until about the seventh of January that my money eventually turned up, but it was too late then. The show had moved on to Valencia and I was never to see them again.

It was a few days after the ice show had left that Castillito told me that he had written to a friend of his, Jose Moya, in Linares, a small mining town in the heart of Andalucian bull-breeding country and the town in which the great Manolete had been killed. My manager suggested that we should go to Linares and Moya would arrange for me to meet some bull-breeders so that I might have a chance of practising with live animals on the ranches.

We took the night train to Baeza, the nearest station to Linares. Arriving there in the early hours of the morning, we had to wait until 7.30 a.m. for the first tram to our destination. It was bitterly cold, so we decided to spend our time in the only warm place in sight, a small café outside the station. We entered the café and ordered steaming hot coffee and large glasses of brandy. Although it was about 4 a.m. the bar was packed with men, mostly shepherds and itinerant horse dealers.

The tram when it eventually started, some twenty minutes late, creaked and groaned as it climbed towards Linares, passing through profusions of multi-coloured wild crocuses. The air was keen and clear. On approaching the outskirts of the town, Castillito, who had seemed half-asleep, suddenly came to life.

"That is the *Hospital Municipal* where poor Manolete died," he said pointing to the left. Following the direction of his finger I saw a large red building set in a beautiful garden. It looked more like an English public school than a hospital. I could imagine Manolete lying there knowing that he was dying and facing death with the same tranquillity with which he had faced the bulls during his life. I could see him crying out to Dr. Jimenez Guinea, "Don Luis, I can't see, I can't see," just before kindly unconsciousness gave his body relief from the agony it was suffering.

I was still thinking about Manolete when the tram rumbled to a halt in a palm-dotted square in the centre of Linares.

"*Vamos*," said Castillito. "This is it."

I spotted the bullring over on the far side of the square.

"That is the ring where Manolete was killed?" I enquired.

"Yes, but you will see enough of it soon. We must go and find Jose Moya first of all, then we will get fixed up in an hotel."

Castillito led the way down the main street to the "Regina", a café at the bottom corner.

"We'll have some coffee here first and enquire where we can find Jose. This is the café frequented by the bullfighters and the bullfight enthusiasts around here," Castillito told me.

We ordered coffee and Castillito asked the barman where we could find Jose Moya. At that very moment the man we were seeking entered the cafe. Castillito greeted his old friend warmly, introduced me and then, when we had finished our coffee, suggested that we went to the bullring.

In the bullring several young fellows were practising and Jose Moya called them over to introduce them and explain that I would be coming every morning to join in the practice sessions. A good crowd of chaps, they promised to help me and later I made particularly good friends of two of them, Enrique Vera and Vicente Escribano, both from Valencia.

The news of my arrival quickly spread and a reporter and photographer from the local press arrived to get a story. They took a photograph of the other boys showing me the exact spot in the ring where Manolete had been killed. I was very pleased with this publicity but the pleasure was soon to be spoiled.

That evening Castillito went off to see some friends of his and promised to meet me at the hotel later. I waited for him until dinner time but he did not appear, so I dined alone. After eating, I went in search of him. Going from bar to bar I could find no sign of my manager but I did encounter Vicente Escribano who told me that he had seen Castillito staggering into the café "Regina". I hurried to the café and there, to my horror, was Castillito, drunk and unconscious, sprawled across a table. I shook him harshly and helping him to his feet led him to the hotel. I was furious that this should have happened, especially as the "Regina" was the café frequented by the local bullfighting fraternity.

Owing to this incident, Castillito and I broke up our *torero-*manager partnership although we remained good friends otherwise. This left me in an unfortunate predicament, stranded in Linares with practically no money to live on and no one to turn to.

The practice sessions in the bullring every morning kept me very occupied. The other *aspirantes* patiently coached me and I progressed rapidly. We rigged up a *carreton*—a bull's head mounted on a bicycle wheel, which by means of two handles is pushed and made to simulate a bull. In place of the big muscle on the neck we had a slab of cork into which we practised placing the *banderillas*. Behind this slab of cork was a slit to represent the spot where the sword should enter.

Taking it in turns to use the *carreton*, we would pair up, one being the *matador* and the other pushing the "bull", then after half an hour we would change places. I found that I learned just as much by being the bull as by being the bull-fighter. I was able to see the whole thing from the bull's angle and saw why it was that the bull would follow the lures instead of attacking the man's body. I could see why it is that the bull-fighter must always be on the offensive and always move forward into what is known as the bull's terrain. This was a turning point in my training. Until this moment I knew how the bull would react to certain movements and situations, but I did not know why. Now that I could understand the theory of bullfighting my confidence was increased one hundred per cent.

By now I was fairly proficient with the cape and *muleta* and started to learn how to place the *banderillas* or darts.

It is not obligatory for a *matador* to be able to place the darts but if he can, it enhances his popularity with the crowd. Nowadays most *matadores* leave this job to their assistants, the *banderilleros*, whose duty it is to get the sticks placed as quickly and efficiently as possible without too much of a show. Since Carlos Arruza the Mexican *matador* retired, there are no *matadores* who excel in this branch of taurine art.

It didn't come easily to me. I found some difficulty in placing them *al quarteo*—the method in which the man runs in an arc across the line of the bull's charge and then, as they meet, spins on his toes and leaning across the horns fixes the darts in the animal's shoulders. I turned too slowly and consequently received many a hard knock from the horns of the *carreton*.

However, in placing them *al quiebro* I was more efficient. In this method the bullfighter, a dart in each hand, stands in front of the bull inciting the beast to charge him; then when it is about six feet away, he sways out with his body and one foot, deflecting the bull's charge. When the horns almost reach his body the man sways back to his original position and places the darts in the animal's shoulder as it hurtles past. This method is very beautiful to watch and appears to be dangerous to an extreme. It is in fact fairly simple to execute, providing the bullfighter keeps a cool head.

The most important thing that I learned at this period was how to effect the swordthrust; "the moment of truth". It is by the sincerity with which he goes in for the kill, rather than by the result he achieves, that a *matador* is judged, but the public will not stand too many misses. Apart from the lack of elegance, they abhor butchery. The crowd will forgive him for striking the bone and not making a proper thrust providing he goes over the horns exposing his body as he does so.

Watching the other boys practising the kill and getting the sword down into the slit on the *carreton* made it appear easy. Then I tried. Vicente Escribano instructed me.

"Stand profile to the bull," he said. "That's right. Now raise your right arm across your chest and sight down the blade of the sword."

I did as I was told.

"Raise your elbow more, so that your forearm and the sword make a straight line," he continued. "Push your left arm out in front of you and slightly to your right so that you are crossing your arms. That's right."

Vicente Escribano took the handles of the *carreton*.

"Now," he signalled.

Pushing the *muleta* out in front and across my body in order to lead the horns past me, I leaned forward and thrust with the sword.

"*Ay! Me cago en tus huesos!*" screamed Vicente. "You've killed me."

He was dancing wildly on the sand and blood was pouring from his hand.

"I am sorry, Vicente," I exclaimed. "What happened?"

"What happened?" he cried. "Can't you see what happened? You ran the sword into my hand. You must have closed your eyes or something. The sword hit the *carreton* about a foot wide of the right place and glanced off into my hand."

"I am sorry," I repeated. "May I try again?"

"Not with me, thank you," replied Vicente.

He turned and called to one of the small boys who were always hanging around in the hope of being allowed to borrow a cape or a *muleta* in order to try a few passes.

"*Chico!* Come here and take the *carreton* for El Ingles here," ordered Vicente. Then he turned to me. "You had better do it in slow motion this time and be careful, otherwise we are going to run out of bulls."

I retrieved the sword and the young boy took the handles of the *carreton*. Taking up position between the horns again, I signalled that I was ready. The boy started to move towards me pushing the bull's head before him. I repeated the same actions as before. This time the sword point struck the *carreton* some six inches wide of the mark.

"You will never do it like that," said Escribano. "You are watching the horns. You mustn't. You must watch the point of the sword and the spot where the sword is to enter."

After a couple more attempts I managed to get the sword into the proper place. I could then see what I had been doing wrong. During the course of a bullfight the *matador* watches the bull's head, and in particular the horns. He gauges his distance from the points of the horns, but at the moment of killing he must disregard the horns entirely and watch only the spot where the sword is to enter. I realised then why the Spaniards call it "the moment of truth", for the bullfighter must throw himself on to the bull heedless of the danger. It is the moment in which a *matador's* courage is tested to the ultimate degree and decides the standard of his worth.

My training was now more interesting and more varied. Gone were the days when I would only practise one pass until my arms ached so that I could hardly hold a cape. Now the long periods of swinging a cape or *muleta* were interspersed with practising nailing *banderillas* and making the *estocadas*, as the swordthrust is called.

As my knowledge and style improved, so my economic situation deteriorated. With the other lads I would wander out into the country to see what we could scrounge. Occasionally we would forage in the market and I became quite adept at "borrowing" from the stalls whilst the owners were not looking. One day it was decided that we would filch some meat, and that one should take it whilst the others distracted the butcher's attention. We drew lots to see who was to be the culprit. It fell to me. Off we went to the market, making our way to the butcher's stall. Surveying the spread I spotted a huge lump of steak right in front and whilst my confederates chatted to the butcher, I grabbed it and stuffed it inside my shirt. However, it turned out to be much larger than I had expected, about a yard long and about two inches thick, so I pulled in my stomach and let the meat down into my trouser leg, tucking the upper end under my belt.

Our mission completed, we made our way to a tavern where the owner, who at one time in his youth had hoped to become a bullfighter, had a soft spot for lads in our position. The short journey there was one of the most uncomfortable walks that I ever had in my life. The meat was hanging well below my knees and although cold and clammy as only meat can be, I was so conscious of it that it was burning a hole in my trousers.

Pronouncing the dedication of my first bull to Don Manuel Gomez, British Vice-Consul in La Linea. (*Below*) The end of the fight and my first experience of being carried shoulder high. (*Photos: Perez-Ponce.*)

(*Above*) A *veronica*, the basis of a *matador's* repertoire with the cape. (*Photo: Perez-Ponce.*) (*Below*) A *natural*, the left-handed pass on which a *matador's* work with the *muleta* is judged. (*Photo: Baker.*)

We arrived safely at the tavern and told the proprietor of our exploit. He asked for the meat, and never have I seen anyone look more surprised than he when I dived my hand under my shirt and slowly withdrew the length of steak. In exchange for a piece of it, he prepared us a meal and threw in a good measure of wine.

Thus we lived. Some days we would go without food of any form and then dine off a chicken or some other luxury "loaned" by some unsuspecting farmer. In order to have an occasional smoke we would buy a single cigarette and it would be passed from mouth to mouth.

To earn myself a little pocket money I used to go with Vicente Escribano selling stockings. Vicente received a regular supply from Valencia and together we would travel from village to village selling them. It was necessary to get to the markets fairly early in order to find a good pitch. Once found, we would open the suitcase and arrange the stockings on the ground.

We had several formulae for attracting a crowd. When trade was bad I would stand and shout in Spanish, "You are lucky to find me here today, ladies. I represent the famous English stocking house of Pim, Pam and Pum of London. This afternoon I am off back to London to buy more of these famous stockings. Look, here is my ticket for the airplane." I would then wave an old envelope or a piece of paper for all to see. It was probably my accent that attracted them for nearly always a good crowd would collect. If this did not work I would wait until an old woman approached and offer her a pair of stockings at a ridiculously low price which she could not possibly refuse. Then, when she handed the money to me I would say that she should pay Vicente, my partner. Vicente would then tell her that the stockings cost twice as much. This would start an argument. Woman's insatiable curiosity would then be our ally, for immediately a huge crowd would gather to find what the fuss was about and sales would flourish. Later we would give the old woman her stockings as a present and bless her for having helped trade.

So as not to waste precious money on fares, we used to travel without tickets. There were several ways of doing this, either by riding the rods—sitting on the axles under the carriages—riding on the carriage roofs, or riding inside the train and moving from lavatory to lavatory. This last method we used only in bad weather. Sometimes, when people we knew were travelling on the train, we would lie under their seats with their luggage piled in front of us. This hiding place was the least comfortable of all but it was the safest. Once, after a day at Cordoba market, we were returning to Linares on the roof of a train when the train pulled up unexpectedly at a wayside station. Two *Guardia Civil*—two travel on every train—alighted, then climbed up on to the roof of the carriage where we were perched and ordered us down. Evidently they had spotted our shadows as we squatted on the carriage roof. After cuffing us pretty severely they left us on the station platform to look after ourselves and find our own way back to Linares. It was a long walk.

In this way I spent some two months in Linares but I was still no nearer my goal. The *tientas* were in progress but I could never manage to find out beforehand where and when they were being held. The bull-breeders always try to keep their *tientas* a secret, to restrain would-be bullfighters from miles around from congregating on their ranches in the hope of being allowed to make a few passes with the calves.

My only close contact with a bull at this period was when Vicente Escribano and I broke into the Linares slaughterhouse one evening, after having been tipped off that a young bull was enclosed there which had been rejected from a herd of fighting-bulls as being not suitable for the bullring. We scaled the wall at the back of the slaughterhouse and into the corrals.

Alone in one of the smaller corrals we found it. A two-year-old, and jet black all over. On hearing us approach it turned and faced us. Having no cape with us we took off our jackets and improvised with these.

Vicente went in first whilst I stood by ready to step in and help should he get into difficulties. At first the bull would only make short rushes and then back away, but Vicente kept in front of the horns all the time, and in doing so made the animal more confident. In a short time it was attacking well and Vicente made some pretty good passes; then he told me to try. I folded my jacket in half and, using it as a *muleta*, managed to do some fairly good *naturales*, passes in which the bullfighter makes the bull go round and round him. In one pass I must have moved the jacket away from the bull a little too fast for it stopped dead half-way through, with its horns right in front of my stomach. Without thinking I brought the jacket forward again and it continued its charge. Accidentally I had split the pass into two parts. Later, Vicente told me how good my action had been; it showed that my reflexes were quicker than my thoughts.

More weeks went past and still there was no sign of my being invited to a *tienta*. I was getting tired of the life I was leading. I was tired of the hunger and lack of money, so I decided to return to La Linea again and ask Adolfo Beaty's advice.

As soon as we had enough cash for two third-class tickets on the mail train, Vicente and I left for La Linea.

5

ARRIVING at La Linea, I made straight for the Vice-Consulate and sought out Adolfo Beaty. He appeared pleased to see me again and I recounted all that had happened during the last six months.

"I think I shall have to go back to England after all," I told him. "It doesn't look as if I will ever get to a *tienta*, and without that chance to show what I can do, how can I ever hope to get a professional fight?"

"Well, it looks as if fate has taken a hand in guiding you here, Vincent," Adolfo said. "This afternoon Don Juan Gallardo is holding a *tienta* at his ranch and you can come with me. Do you have a cape and *muleta*?"

I replied that I had bought a cape and *muleta* in Madrid.

This was to be my big chance, for nearly everyone invited to watch the *tienta* would be connected with bullfighting in some way. If I put on a good show I might get an invitation to partake in another, or even be offered a real contract to fight in public.

After lunch Adolfo picked Vicente and myself up in his car and we set off for the ranch of Juan Gallardo. As we sped over the road towards Algeciras, my mind went back to the night when with Manolo and El Niño I had walked all the way to Gallardo's ranch to fight a bull by moonlight. I told Adolfo of that escapade.

"If I had known about it I would never have allowed you to go, Vincent," he admonished. "Keep quiet about it when we

68

get to the ranch. If Juan Gallardo finds out about it, he'll have you thrown off the place."

Soon the car turned off on to the track that led to the ranch-house itself. As we pulled up in front of the *patio* our host came forward to greet us.

Juan Gallardo was a very amiable man in his early thirties and had a rather boyish face that beamed with enthusiasm. He told us that the *tienta* was about ready to begin and that most of the guests were already down at the little practice ring.

As we followed him down to join the others we saw the cowboys riding in, herding the young cows that were to be tested that afternoon.

Entering the ring from the large gate that gave directly on to the open pasture, I saw that there were about twenty guests, most of whom sat atop the white horn-pitted wall of the ring. The *picador* was there and was adjusting the straps that supported the horse's padding. He mounted and then tried the balance of the lance with which he was going to *pic* the cows. The *pic* in this case is a much smaller one than that used in real bullfights and has a very tiny point. As I stood watching, I could hear the shouts of the *vaqueros* and the bells of the steers as the cows were herded and separated in the corrals.

Juan Gallardo motioned us to take our places behind the barriers. Vicente Escribano and I took the one nearest the big door through which we had entered the ring. The rancher stood near the corrals and Adolfo Beaty with him. The *picador* took up his position between our barrier and the door from the corrals. The other two bullfighters present, Ramon Cervera and Chiclanero, took up theirs on the opposite side. Juan Gallardo signalled us to keep quiet and then called to one of the *vaqueros* to let in the first cow.

The door swung open and she tore into the ring, then pulled up to survey the scene. Nobody moved. Juan Gallardo watched intently to see if she would attack the horse without being provoked. She did not. He shouted to the *picador* to move nearer and call the cow to attack. The *picador* urged the horse forward a few steps and called out to the cow in the same manner that the bullfighters call to the bull in a bullfight. The cow pawed the ground and shook her head. I knew this was a bad sign; she was bluffing. Again the *picador* moved a little nearer and called: "*Aha vaca, mira bonita.*" This time she took a step backwards and then suddenly charged the horse. As her horns reached the padding round the horse, the *picador* shot out the lance and sunk the point into her shoulders. The effect was electric. The cow leapt backwards, bellowed, and ran off round the ring. Juan Gallardo called to Ramon Cervera, who was the senior bullfighter present, to try to get her to attack his cape. Ramon stepped out from behind the shelter and called to the cow, but as he shook his cape she shied away from it.

"Let her go," shouted the bull-breeder; "she's no good."

And making a note in his notebook, marking her for the slaughterhouse, he called to me to let her out. The door opened outwards and as I swung it open I stood behind it until the cow was far enough out on to the pasture for her not to attack me. As soon as she saw the opening she ran out and escaped to the peace of the range. I re-entered the ring and after closing the door behind me took up my position behind the shelter again.

For the second time the door to the corrals was swung open and the next cow was let in. This one trotted in quietly and then, on spotting the horse, charged straight across the ring and attacked it. The *picador* drove the *pic* into her shoulders but the cow insisted under the steel and kept hooking at the padding of the horse. Juan Gallardo signalled to Ramon Cervera to make his *quite** and take the cow away from the

---

* *Quite*, pronounced kee-tay, is the act of taking away the bull from the horse or from a fallen bullfighter. In the first case, the *quites* form the first act of the bullfight, the *matadores* taking it in turns to take the bull away

horse. At the *tientas* the *toreros* do their *quites* and take the cows for the final work with the *muleta* in order of seniority, as in formal bullfights. A *matador's* seniority is based on the length of time he has been fighting as a professional or from the date of his presentation in the Madrid bull-ring.

Ramon ran out to the side of the horse and with his cape distracted the cow from her attack. He did not make any fancy passes but simply led her to the distance from the horse that the bull-breeder indicated. It was imperative that the cow should not be tired unnecessarily until it was clear how often she would attack the *picador*. Ramon did a *recorte*, a pass which is designed to cut short the animal's charge and fix it in one spot.

The *picador* again called to the cow, and without any hesitation she re-attacked. This procedure was repeated several times until altogether the cow had attacked the horse and received the steel of the *pic* in her shoulders ten times. Finally Juan Gallardo called out: "All right, she's had enough; you can take her with the *muleta*, Ramon."

Ramon Cervera took his *muleta* and began a series of passes with it which he continued until the cow was almost too tired to attack. This gave the bull-breeder a chance to see how well she would attack and for how long. Eventually he called out to me to let her go. I opened the gate but this time the cow had to be caped out into the pasture before she would give up the fight. She was an extremely brave animal and would be used for breeding fighting stock. It is said that a fighting bull inherits its bravery from its mother and its size and general type from its father.

Taking them in order of our seniority I knew that Vicente Escribano's animal would be the third and mine the fourth.

from the horse. Each *matador* tries to outdo his companion in the quality and variety of passes that he employs to form his *quite*.

It was when Vicente had finished with his animal that an amusing incident occurred. I had opened the door to let his cow out on to the pasture, and as before, I pulled the door wide open and stood behind it until the animal was well out of range. This cow came out all right but after going about ten feet she suddenly decided to turn around and come back into the ring again. I was helpless to prevent her from doing so. Her disappearance inside was followed by a yell. Evidently, Vicente Escribano had been bending down to adjust one of his boots and had not seen the cow re-enter the ring, but she had seen him. The next thing he knew was that something had hit him in the behind and he was flat on his face in the dirt. Luckily he escaped with only a rip in the seat of his trousers but it took some explaining later as nobody would believe that he had not been running away.

The fourth cow turned out to be very brave and after she had attacked the *picador* several times Juan Gallardo called out for me to try her with the *muleta*.

Picking up my *muleta* and spreading it over a stick which I used to take the place of the sword, I stepped towards her, trembling with excitement as each step took me nearer those horns. I decided to start with a *pase de la muerte*, a pass in which the *matador* must stand still and erect, with his feet firmly together, incite the animal to charge and then, when the horns reach the cloth of the *muleta*, raise the lure, allowing the animal to pass beneath it, its horns scraping his chest. I did two of these passes and then, noticing that this cow hooked in closely with her left horn, I decided to take her with the right-handed passes called *en redondo* in which the *matador* makes the animal pass round and round him in a clockwise direction. My little lady followed these well and after a series of them I sent her away from me with a *pase de pecho*—a chest pass.

The applause that followed this series encouraged me and

I prepared to begin another *faena*.* Again I sited the cow for right-handed passes, but this time I dropped my hand holding the *muleta* a little lower, so that I should pass the horns closer to my body. It was a little too low. The cow charged and tossed me, catching my left hand against my leg as she did so. I felt a searing pain in my finger and knew that the bone was fractured.

Immediately the other bullfighters ran out to me and, caping the cow away, helped me to my feet.

"Are you all right?" enquired Ramon Cervera.

"Yes thanks, just a little bruised, I think," I assured him.

"You'd better take it easy for a while and then try again in a minute when your next turn comes," he advised.

Following his advice, I slipped in behind my shelter and stood there waiting until my next animal was let into the ring. Taking part in any *quite* was out of the question; my finger was too painful for me to hold a cape. When my turn came again for me to work with the *muleta* I had to use my right hand the whole time. This was particularly annoying as I was very keen to try some left-handed *naturales*, the important basis of a *matador's* repertoire with the *muleta*.

Daylight was leaving the Andalucian countryside as the last cow was let loose on the pasture to return to the herd, and we made our way to the ranch-house where Juan Gallardo had some sherry and a snack prepared for his guests. Adolfo Beaty and I walked together.

"Well," I asked him, "how did I make out?"

"Not bad. Not bad at all. You held yourself much too stiff but your timing and execution of the passes was fine. You must remember that you are not a soldier on parade but a bullfighter.

* *Faena.* In this sense, a series of passes with the *muleta* which a *matador* makes in the third and final act of a bullfight. A *matador* endeavours to create a number of different *faenas*, each containing a series of beautiful and varied passes.

73

Just relax a little more and loosen up." Beaty encouraged. "You'll make it all right. I think you surprised some of the people present today."

As we entered the house, Juan Gallardo came up and offered us some sherry and smoked ham.

"How do you feel, *chico*?" he asked.

"Fine, Don Juan, fine," I replied.

"The cow did not hurt you then?" he questioned.

"No, just a shaking, that's all. Those little cows were too small to do any real damage," I said.

"Don't you believe it," said my host; "I have seen several *toreros* get *cornadas* from cows no bigger than those you fought today."

A *cornada* was, I knew, a serious and deep horn wound as opposed to a *puntazo* which is a not very deep wound made with just the *punta* or point of the horn.

"You must relax a little more," he continued, repeating Adolfo Beaty's advice, "and follow through more at the end of each pass. You tend to bring the animal back on to your body."

Adolfo had to be back in La Linea early so we bade Juan Gallardo farewell, and after thanking him for having invited me to the *tienta* I followed Adolfo into the car. My finger was throbbing madly by now and I was anxious to get back to La Linea. Vicente Escribano was very quiet on the return journey. He seemed annoyed over the torn trousers incident. We alighted from the car at the little hotel where Vicente and I were staying and arranged to meet Adolfo later that evening at the *Casino*—*Casino* being the popular name for the *Club Mercantil*, the business men's club.

Straightway I had a good look at my finger. This was the first opportunity I had had of examining it and estimating the amount of damage done. The middle joint was now exceedingly swollen and very stiff. I couldn't afford to go to a doctor so I found a couple of pieces of straight wood and using them for splints bandaged my finger as tight as I could bear. Then I lay down to rest a while before going out.

When I saw Adolfo at the *Casino* he was sitting with a crowd of bullfight enthusiasts.

"*Olá*, Vicente," he greeted me. This was the first time that Adolfo had used the Spanish version of my name and it pleased me, as I realised that at last I was being accepted into the intimate bullfighting circle.

"We were just discussing your performance this afternoon. You created quite a good impression. It has been suggested that you should have someone like Pajarero—he is an old *ex-torero* who lives here in town—to give you some lessons so that you can polish up your style a bit."

"Do you think he will take me on?" I asked.

"Yes. He is a good chap and interested in youngsters. We'll see him tomorrow," said Adolfo.

The next day Adolfo took me along to see Pajarero. We found him in his rented room not far from the Vice-Consulate. The walls of his room were covered with faded photographs of himself in the bullring. On one wall hung a frame full of yellowed press cuttings. Relics of a past and glorious youth. A story of a bygone *taurine* era.

Pajarero assented to Adolfo's suggestion and promised to take me to the bullring for an hour every day to improve my technique. We made arrangements to meet later that day for the first lesson.

On the way to the bullring that evening we collected a small boy who agreed to play bull for me for the sum of 50 *centimos*—about a penny—an hour. There was an old pair of horns kept permanently at the bullring for the use of anybody who might care to practise with them. The little boy was very enthusiastic, so much so in fact, that as I was doing one pass he chopped upwards with the horns in the manner of a bull

75

and stuck the point of one of the horns into my arm. I bear the scar to this day.

After a week I discarded the bandages and splints on my finger but found that I couldn't bend it at all. It was still very painful when I used it, and very inconvenient in training.

Pajarero was a proficient professor and kept me hard at it. So hard in fact that I began to get bored. He would make me concentrate on just one particular pass and keep me at it for a solid hour; but the outcome was worth my while. I became far more supple and more natural.

The lessons had been going on for about a fortnight when Adolfo told me that a *tienta* was being held on the coming Saturday at the nearby ranch of the Vazquez brothers, Don Fernando and Don Ramon. He told me that a great deal would depend on how I had progressed since the *tienta* at Gallardo's ranch.

With the exception of Vicente Escribano who had returned to Valencia, the same bullfighters, Ramon Cervera and Chiclanero, were there, and as before we took our places in the *tienta* ring and awaited the entry of the cows.

The first group to be tested were all five-year-olds that had been previously tested and caped. Beaty whispered to me to remain where I was until the younger animals were brought in. These older cows would be too dangerous for me with my very limited experience.

Eventually a younger animal was brought in and it was my turn to fight. I made every pass that I could think of, using both my hands, either singly or together. When Don Fernando Vazquez decided that I had had enough time with the animal, he told me to lead her with the cape out and on to the pasture. Somehow or other I didn't allow enough room for her to pass me in the gateway and she tossed me against the wall, tearing my trousers in several places. But worst of all, she caught my bad finger. It was agonising and I had to bite my lip to prevent myself from crying out.

Up at the ranch-house whilst we were having the sherry and snacks that customarily follow the *tienta*, Fernando Vasquez approached me and congratulated me on my showing.

Turning to Adolfo Beaty he said: "He will soon be ready for a real fight, Adolfo. You'll have to bill him in La Linea."

"Yes, I don't think it will be long now, Vicente, before you can make your professional debut," said Adolfo.

I felt so excited at this thought that I forgot about my finger.

Two days later, Adolfo approached me. "How would you like to fight in La Linea bullring on Sunday? Miguel Campos and Pepe Chapi will be fighting bulls from Juan Belmonte's ranch. So far I haven't signed anyone to be third *matador*. Do you want it?"

I was nonplussed and for a moment I just could not answer. Then, without thinking, I accepted the offer. At that moment I didn't appreciate the momentous decision I had made.

"By the way, how shall we bill you?" asked Adolfo.

"I think I'll just use my Christian names, Vincent Charles. That should be easy enough for people to remember," I replied.

"That should be all right. We'll call you Vincent Charles *El Ingles*, just to show that you are English; as it is, most people around here seem to know you as *El Ingles*," continued Adolfo.

"Shall I be able to hire a bullfighter's suit and swords and capes and *muletas* and all the other paraphernalia that I shall need?" I asked.

"Yes, don't worry about that, we'll see that you are fixed up all right," replied Adolfo. "But I think you should have a manager now, Vicente," he continued. "You know that boy Miguel Ropero, whose father owns the bar 'Bodega Jerezana'?

77

He would like to manage you. Go and see him and, if you think he'll be all right, ask him to see that you get all the equipment you need."

Following Adolfo's suggestion I went to see Miguel Ropero. He was a youngster a couple of years my senior who had never had any responsibility in his life and who was thrilled at the idea of managing a *torero*. Together we went to Algeciras to see a swordhandler named Pedro Mejias who hired out bull-fighting costumes and equipment. I chose a suit of pale blue, embroidered with silver. Pedro's wife made the necessary alterations to make it fit me properly. I then chose a heavily embroidered dress cape of dark blue silk to set off the lightness of the suit. With Pedro's guidance we selected two heavy fighting capes and two *muletas*. The swordhandler promised to supply a complete set of swords and also to act as sword-handler for me on the day of the fight.

That night, back in my room in La Linea, I lay on my bed tossing sleeplessly, worried about the decision I had taken and what might be the outcome of the coming Sunday's per-formance. Doubts assailed my mind. Was I sufficiently experi-enced yet to appear in public? Would it not be better to wait another month or two? Eventually I got up, dressed, and went for a walk. I walked until daylight.

With the advent of daylight things didn't look so bad, and it was with a sense of pleasant anticipation that I watched the workmen nailing up across the main street the banner announc-ing my forthcoming debut.

Miguel Ropero met me at the café where I was breakfasting and asked how I felt about everything.

"Fine," I told him. "The only thing that is worrying me is whether I shall be able to kill well."

"You'll do it. Don't worry." He tried to reassure me.

"Don't forget, Miguel, I've only practised with a *carreton*. The real thing must be very different," I replied.

"Everyone has to have a first time, Vincent. Providing you do everything the way you've practised, you'll be O.K."

I was not so easily convinced and the thought that I might make a mess of things worried me greatly.

"Miguel, isn't there some way in which I could have a shot at killing with the sword? In the slaughterhouse maybe?" I asked my new manager.

"No, they won't let you do that in the slaughterhouse. For one thing, it would spoil the hide of the animal," replied Miguel. "Just a minute though; maybe we can arrange to buy a bull from Mosquito and you can kill it in the bullring one evening. Wait here a minute and I'll go and telephone the slaughterhouse to see what he says."

Miguel left the table and went to the telephone and I watched as he dialled a number and began to speak. After a while he turned to me and winked, and I guessed that he had managed to arrange something.

Returning to the table he said: "It's all right, Mosquito has agreed to let us have a bull. We'll go to the bullring this evening and you can kill it. You will have to pay the expenses such as transport to the bullring, butcher's fees and for damage done to the hide."

"What do I use for money," I asked.

"Don't worry about it. I'll pay for it and you can pay me back later, when you start earning. That's part of a manager's job," Miguel assured me. I could see that he was thoroughly enjoying his new role and the new-found close contact with the world of *tauromaquia*.

The idea of being able to kill a bull in the bullring without an audience, before making my debut in public, raised my morale enormously and I looked forward with impatience to the evening.

Miguel said: "I think it will be a good idea if we get Pedro, your swordhandler, over here from Algeciras and ask him to bring the suit with him so that you can get the feel of fighting dressed in the heavy costume. You will also be able to practise the ritual; Adolfo Beaty will show you."

It is very important in a bullfight that the traditional pattern of proceedings is closely adhered to, and I was glad of this opportunity to learn and practise things which any Spanish boy would have known from having seen them performed time and time again. I had not seen enough bullfights to have been able to learn the finer points of the rites involved.

At seven o'clock my swordhandler Pedro arrived and we walked to the bullring, as I was to change into the costume there.

Wearing the costume, unfamiliar as it was, and being in the atmosphere of the arena, made me feel as if I had been a professional *torero* for years. Adolfo showed me how to stand like a bullfighter with one leg forward, slightly bent at the knee. Whilst waiting to begin the parade bullfighters usually stand with the left leg forward. In this way they will start off on the right foot which is supposed to be lucky.

After I had practised making the parade across the ring a couple of times, Miguel told me to stand behind the barrier and wait for the bull to be loosed.

The door to the bullpens was swung open and into the ring skipped the bull. It was not what I had been expecting. Usually they tear into the ring like express trains but this one just skipped in, then trotted gaily round the perimeter of the ring. One of the *banderilleros* who was to form part of my *cuadrilla*—team—on Sunday had come along to run the bull for me. He stepped out from the barrier offering his cape to the bull but it just continued circumnavigating the ring.

"It is looking for the way out of here," said Miguel, who was standing beside me. "When it realises there is no escape it will probably start attacking."

"I know it's only a meat bull but I expected it to be fiercer than this," I replied.

80

If the bull did not start attacking I knew that the evening would be a complete waste of time and effort, because I wouldn't be able to get in front of it to make the kill.

"Alfonso will make it attack in a minute," said Miguel indicating the *banderillero*.

Watching the *banderillero* I saw that he kept advancing towards the bull, stamping his foot and then retreating rapidly, hoping to make the animal think that he was afraid. After this procedure had been repeated a few times, the bull lowered its head and charged a few steps. Again the *banderillero* retreated, more slowly this time. Little by little he managed to make the animal charge for longer distances. Never once did he attempt to make it pass him but each time, keeping himself and the cape in front of the horns, he would run backwards, away from it, just keeping the cape in front of its nose. Thus he was giving the bull confidence.

Suddenly he left the bull and came over to where I was standing.

"You will not be able to use the cape, *jefe*.* You had better take the *muleta* and sword and kill it straight away," he said.

My swordhandler handed me the folded *muleta* and the sword. Taking the *muleta* in my left hand, and holding the sword across it with my thumb, I walked over to the front of the presidential box and went through the formality of asking an imaginary president permission to kill. I then followed my *banderillero* over to where the bull was standing.

"Stand behind me," Alfonso whispered. "I'm going to pass it this time and as it comes through you must attract its attention with the *muleta*."

Following his instructions, I stood about nine paces behind him and as he passed the bull with a form of *veronica* I attracted the animal's attention to the *muleta*. I heard my *banderillero* shout "*Ahora!* Now!" and then, sighting along the blade of

* Chief.

81

the sword, I went in to kill as I had done so many times on the *carreton*. The sword entered to the hilt and the bull stood swaying on its feet before crashing to the sand, dead.

"There you are, Vicente, I told you that you'd do it all right," said my manager as we walked home from the bullring.

I was elated.

That night, instead of going to bed, tossing restlessly and then dressing and going out, as I had done every night since accepting the contract to appear in the ring, I decided to walk around until I was so tired that I was sure to sleep. I walked all night. It was amazing that I suffered no ill effects from this. For five days I had been without sleep and still did not feel tired, either physically or mentally. Now there were only twenty-four hours left before the great moment and I knew that I had to get some sleep.

It was Saturday morning and the day before the fight. My manager suggested that I should go over to Gibraltar and let myself be seen there. He said it would be good publicity, so I crossed the border and wandered around Gibraltar during the morning. Big, gaily-coloured posters depicting bulls and bullfighters were all over town. I could not get used to the idea of seeing my name on them. It all seemed a crazy nightmare.

After wandering up and down Main Street a few times, I made my way to the house of my friend Johnny Graham where I was expected for lunch. A false note of gaiety ran through the conversation during the meal and I couldn't help but notice my friends' nervousness. We talked of everything but the morrow's affair.

As we sat in armchairs taking coffee after lunch, I fell asleep and slept solidly until 11 p.m. Feeling very embarrassed on waking, I apologised to my host for my rudeness. He assured me that he didn't mind in the least as I had obviously needed a good rest. I left the house hurriedly and crossed the border just before the frontier gates were closed.

Arriving at La Linea, I was met by a very worried-looking Miguel.

"Where have you been, Vicente?" he demanded.

"In Gibraltar," I replied.

"But what have you been doing? I've had people looking for you all over the place," he said.

"I'm sorry but I've been asleep," I told him.

"Asleep! *Por Dios!* I thought that maybe you had been kidnapped by some of your compatriots who don't like bull-fighting, so that you wouldn't be able to fight tomorrow," continued Miguel.

I couldn't help laughing at my manager's fears. I could just imagine his thoughts, after the big build-up this fight had been given, on suddenly finding that I had apparently disappeared without trace.

"Don't be silly. Nobody would do that," I assured him.

"But I know how the R.S.P.C.A. feel about bullfighting," he went on.

"Not even they would go to such extremes, Miguel. Anyway, forget it. I am here and I'm still feeling very sleepy, so after letting you buy me a cognac for a nightcap, I'm off to bed. I'm working tomorrow, or had you forgotten?"

"Forgotten!" he said. "How could I forget? I'm as scared as you are!"

"Scared? I'm not scared," I retorted.

Indeed after that afternoon's sleep I had woken up to find myself calmer than I had ever been.

Miguel and I had a brandy each and then I went to bed. I slept soundly all night.

6

IT was 11 a.m. when Pedro, my swordhandler, came to
wake me. He laid out the pale blue and silver costume over
a chair in the corner of the bedroom and after seeing that
everything was to his satisfaction, turned to me.

"Are you going to Mass, *jefe*?" he enquired.

Until this moment I hadn't thought about it but it seemed
to be the right thing to do and, after all, I had plenty to pray
for.

"Yes. I'll go to the 11.30 Mass. Have you been yet, Pedro?"
I enquired of him.

"I haven't had time to yet, *jefe*. I'll come with you," he
replied.

I suspected that he had already been, but thought that I
might like to have someone to accompany me. He was right.
I had never been to Mass before and it would be easier having
someone to follow.

We walked down the *Calle Real* towards the little white
church that stood in the square at the end of the street. The
pavements were lined with people sitting at café tables taking
an early *aperitivo*. As we passed I could hear my name being
mentioned and once or twice, out of the corner of my eye, I
caught sight of people pointing in my direction and caught the
words—"*El Ingles que va a torear esta tarde.*"—the Englishman who is going to fight this afternoon. There was evidently
a lot of interest in the coming fight.

When we arrived at the church Mass was already being
said and we had to stand at the back. There was still a steady

84

flow of people entering and soon the church was uncomfortably overcrowded. Looking around me I could not help but notice that to most of the congregation religion seemed more of a habit than a devotion.

The service came to an end and I walked back with Pedro down the *Calle Real* towards the café Anglo-Hispano where we were to await my manager and Adolfo Beaty. Finding ourselves an empty table on the pavement outside the café, we sat down and Pedro called the waiter.

"You'd better have a fruit juice, *jefe*," he said.

"No alcohol?" I asked.

"It's better not to have any. It affects the nervous system even in small quantities," said my swordhandler, "though most *toreros* have a coffee with a tot of cognac in it just before they leave for the ring."

The waiter approached and Pedro ordered two glasses of lemon juice. The facts that Pedro drank lemon juice with me and not wine as he would have preferred, and that he had gone to Mass a second time just to keep me company, were examples of attributes which I came very much to admire in him.

It was with a great deal of impatience that I awaited the arrival of my manager and Adolfo, for they had gone to the bullring for the *sorteo*, the sorting out of the bulls.

The *sorteo* usually takes place around noon on the day of the bullfight. The six bulls to be killed in the afternoon have been brought in from the country and enclosed in the corrals of the bullring. At the appointed hour the *matador's* representatives, usually his manager and senior *banderillero*—known as his confidential *banderillero*—go down to the corrals and with the representatives of the other two *matadores* pair the bulls as near as possible into three equal pairs. Perhaps a big bull will be paired with a small animal, or one with large horns with one with a small pair. After a lot of discussion and argument, the six bulls are paired and the numbers of each pair are written on separate cigarette papers which are then screwed up into tiny balls and dropped into a hat. The hat is shaken and the *banderilleros* draw the papers out according to the seniority of the *matadores* they represent. The bulls are then separated and penned in semi-darkness in order to quieten and rest them. In no way are they starved or provoked before being set loose.

Pedro and I had been sitting at the table about a quarter of an hour when he pointed up the road saying, "Here they come." Following his eyes I saw my manager and Adolfo approaching together with Fernando Naranjo, "Rondeño", who was to be my confidential *banderillero* that afternoon.

I started to get up. "Come on, Pedro," I said to my sword-handler. "Let's go and find out what bulls we've drawn."

"You had better wait here for them to arrive, *jefe*. They will tell us soon enough. You mustn't appear impatient," he said. "*Matadores* are supposed to be above worrying about what bulls they draw."

I took his advice and sat down again to wait for the trio to arrive. On seeing us sitting outside the café, they hurried towards us.

"This is certainly your lucky day, Vicente," began Miguel; "you have drawn the best pair by far."

"A couple of beauties. Horns like this," said Adolfo, crooking his two index fingers inwards to indicate the shape of the horns.

"We'll cut the ears all right this afternoon, *jefe*," Fernando joined in.

Adolfo must have read the look of disbelief in my face for he continued; "Believe me, Vicente, you have nothing to worry about."

Miguel, my manager, as if reading my mind, backed Adolfo up. "I know that we should have said this in any case," he said, "but I swear by all that is holy, Vicente, you have drawn two dream bulls for your debut."

86

Adolfo left us to go to the box office to see how the sale of tickets was progressing. Miguel and Fernando sat down at the table and after ordering wine for themselves, continued describing the two bulls that I was to fight later that day. We had sat there for an hour or more when my swordhandler suggested that I should go to bed and rest until the hour arrived for me to start dressing.

"I had better go and have my lunch now," I said to my swordhandler.

"*Toreros* do not eat on the day of the fight, *jefe*," Pedro replied.

"But why not?" I asked curiously.

"It—er—it is in case of a goring in the stomach," said my swordhandler nervously, stretching out his hand and touching wood as he did so. My surprise at seeing Pedro's nervousness made me forget the implication of his words. I walked back to my room.

Back in the solitude, doubts and fears again began to crowd my mind and the full realisation of what the afternoon might bring dawned upon me. I pictured all the gorings that I had seen and tried to imagine how it would feel to have a horn ripping through my flesh. I wondered how I would react to an injury. It had always amazed me whenever I had seen bull-fighters being gored, how unworried they appeared to be. I thought of a boy I had known, Luis Miguel Sanz, who had been killed by a bull; gored through the heart, some months previously.

That would be the best way to die, I decided; it would be quick and probably painless. But what if I should lose a limb or even an eye? It had happened often enough. I began to feel sick and getting up from my bed, I went outside to the lavatory. Somehow my bladder had become weak. That was the third time that I had relieved myself in the last half an hour.

A radio blaring out from a nearby house played a *pasodoble torero*, music of the bullring, and this had a stimulating effect on me. Like the feeling of intense patriotism and national pride one feels on hearing a Guards' band play a stirring march. The music stopped and a shrill feminine voice began announcing the afternoon's *corrida*.

"This afternoon in La Linea a grand bullfight. Six brave bulls from the ranch of Don Juan Belmonte for the following bullfighters: Miguel Campos of La Linea, Pepe Chapi of Sevilla and Vincent Charles (she pronounced it Vicente Charlays) of London, the first Englishman to become a bullfighter. Do not miss this great . . . etc. . . . etc. . . ."

It seemed strange and unreal to hear the fight announced like that over the radio. It sounded like somebody announcing a freak show. Come to think of it, that's what it is, I thought, a bloody freak show. People won't be coming to see what I do, but what I don't do. I got up and went to the lavatory again.

Returning to the bed, I lay down and lit another cigarette. How many had I smoked since Pedro had left me? The ashtray was full of stubs, some of them two inches in length. My hands were sweating so much that they soaked the cigarettes and made them fall apart along the seams.

The radio was blaring out the announcement again when the door of my room opened and Pedro came in.

"They're a bit late," he said, indicating the radio. "The tickets are all sold. It's going to be a full house today, *jefe*."

At that moment there was a knock on the door. Pedro opened it to admit the barber who had arrived to shave me.

Whilst I was being shaved, my swordhandler arranged an altar on the dressing-table. He placed photographs of various holy *Virgens* and a figurette of *La Macarena* who from her church in Sevilla stretches a guarding hand to all bullfighters. Pedro placed three candles before the altar and lighted them.

When the barber had finished shaving me, the complicated

process of dressing began. First of all Pedro made me put on my *montera*, the black hat worn by bullfighters. He then selected a tuft of hair at the back of my head, just below the lower edge of the hat; to this he would later fix the traditional pigtail. Twisting the strands, he slipped them into a split screw, the ends of which he tightened together with a nut. The reason for attaching the clip before combing my hair was to prevent it slipping once my hair had been brilliantined.

Next I put on my vest and the white linen underpants which reached to just below my knees and two pairs of stockings, a white cotton pair first to prevent the following pink silk pair from wrinkling. These I held taut under my pants whilst Pedro tightened the tapes below my knees to hold the stockings in place.

Now came the difficult part of wriggling into the skin-tight *taleguilla*, the figure-moulding breeches. I sat on the edge of the bed, stiff-legged, while Pedro pulled the *taleguilla* over my feet and up my legs. I then stood up, and with Pedro holding the back and the barber the front of my breeches they lifted me off the floor and shook me down into them. Pedro then took a towel, twisted it, and told me to sit astride it. Then he and the barber each held an end whilst I wriggled until my breeches fitted like a tight glove. At last they were on, and I slipped my feet into the black pumps whilst Pedro tightened the laces on the breeches just below my knees. The lacing up of the breeches is most important; they must be laced to just the right pressure. Too much and the circulation is restricted, too little and no support is given to the bullfighter's legs and he feels insecure. All these details have a psychological effect on the man in the ring, just as much as has his physical fitness. Naturally a bullfighter can never hope to compete with a bull in strength nor, as it is his obligation to stand still unless he is placing the *banderillas*, is it necessary for him to be agile. However, the fact that he feels strong and agile gives him the will to dominate the bull. It's just a question of wills. When Pedro had finished lacing my trousers he tied the ribbons on my pumps into neat bows.

The worst was now over. All I had to do was to put on shirt, sash, waistcoat and jacket. First the shirt of fine white linen with lace and frills down the front, with which I wore a red tie about an inch wide throughout its length. After buttoning the *taleguilla*, first the inside fly which is placed to one side and which acts as a sort of built-in support, then the outside fly, Pedro helped me into the red sash which he passed once around my waist, tying it in front and intertwining the ends round the lower part of my braces; then into my waistcoat, and I was nearly ready. I had been so busy that I had forgotten my fears. I lit a cigarette but noticed that my hand shook slightly. It was now nearly time to leave and I awaited with impatience the arrival of the car that was to take me to the bull-ring. Pedro slipped out of the door and returned shortly with a cup of black coffee and a tot of brandy. I poured the brandy into the coffee and drank it down hurriedly and then while Pedro was helping me into the stiff and heavily embroidered bolero jacket that completed the costume, there was a knock on the door to announce that the car was waiting.

Picking up my dress cape and hat, I said a silent prayer before the altar, then, carrying my cape over my arm and my hat in my hand, I went out to the car, Pedro following with the leather box containing the fighting capes and *muletas* and the leather sword case.

I sat in the back seat of the car between my manager and Pedro. A small crowd had gathered on the pavement to watch us leave and, as we moved off, an olive-skinned gipsy girl, carrying a baby, leaned forward, touched me on the shoulder and assured me that everything would go well.

We turned into the road that led to the bullring. The pavements were thronged with people as indeed was most of the roadway. A steady stream of humanity slowly flowing towards a common goal.

We passed one of the huge posters announcing the fight and I couldn't stop myself looking at it to see my name again. It still seemed unreal. Surely that could not be me, billed to kill two bulls on this Sunday afternoon of the 5th June, 1949? Surely it was a mad dream and any moment I would wake up and life would be simple once again.

The car moved slowly because of the press of bodies we had to pass through. People kept waving and shouting to me, wishing me good luck, and I thought how false they probably were; that in reality they were all going to see what sort of a fiasco I would produce. Suddenly I realised we had reached the bullring and were outside the gate where the bullfighters enter. My *cuadrilla*, who had gone ahead, were just alighting from their vehicle and waiting for me to lead the way. We shook hands and greeted each other, then I led the way into the *patio de caballos*, the courtyard where the bullfighters await the signal to make the parade across the ring. The door through which we came into the bullring was set midway between the *patio de caballos* and the yard where the bulls were butchered, and I caught a glimpse of two men from the slaughterhouse sharpening their skinning and cleaving knives in preparation for the coming afternoon's work.

Someone called my name. It was Pepe Perez Ponce, the photographer. He wanted to take some photographs before the fight started. I walked stiff-legged to where he was standing with Miguel Campos and Pepe Chapi, passing as I did so the mule team which was already in harness to drag the carcasses from the ring. The mules looked splendid, their bell-covered harness gleaming, and brand-new red and yellow pennants fluttering from their collars. I greeted Miguel Campos and Pepe Chapi and we wished each other luck for the afternoon's performance.

Three photographers tried to lead me to different positions for photographs and everybody, it seemed, wanted to be in the picture. I have no idea how many photographs were taken but a good length of film must have been used.

Pedro, who had disappeared into the *callejon*, the narrow corridor that runs round the bullring between spectators and the arena and in which the bullfighters and bullring attendants stand when not in action, reappeared and told me it was time for me to put on my dress cape.

Unfolding it, I swung it on to my left shoulder and pulling the rear corner under my right arm, grasped both points firmly in my left hand whilst Pedro gathered up the lower edge and tucked it up under my left forearm, tight against my body, leaving my right arm swinging free at my side. I had to carry my hat in this hand during the parade, out of deference to the public of La Linea, this being my presentation in their bullring.

I took up my position between Miguel Campos and Pepe Chapi and our *cuadrillas* formed up in columns behind us, the bullring attendants and the mule teams bringing up the rear. It was a tense moment.

At last the trumpet sounded and the gates in front of us were flung open, revealing a blaze of yellow sand surrounded by a seething sea of faces. The vivid blue and cloudless sky formed a canopy high above our heads.

The photographers dashed out in front and took last-minute pictures before the parade began. Then it was Miguel Campos saying, "*Que Dios reparta la suerte. Vamos.*"—May God share out the luck. Let's go. We all muttered "*Suerte*"—luck. The band struck up with a *pasodoble* and we swung out across the ring.

It seemed even more dream-like now. I felt as if my feet weren't touching the ground. I made a conscious effort to emulate the bullfighters I had watched, marching slightly pigeon-toed and swinging easily from the hips. I began to feel the part.

Arriving below the presidential box we bowed to the president, who in this case was the local chief of police, and then made our way to where our respective swordhandlers were waiting ready to give us the heavy fighting capes. We slipped off our dress capes and handed them to our swordhandlers, who in turn handed them up to friends in the front seats who would spread them out over the barrier dividing the seats from the *callejon*.

Opening our fighting capes we tried them in a couple of passes to see how they handled and what wind there was, if any. Then we slipped in behind the plank shelter and through the opening in the main barrier which it covered, and thence into the *callejon*. The bullring attendants, called *areneros*, were smoothing over the sand that had been disturbed during the parade. One man shovelled up a heap of dung dropped by one of the mules.

Miguel Campos was due to take the first bull and with his *banderillero de confianza* by his side he moved into the space between the plank shelter and the barrier.

He did well with his animal and made a clean kill and afterwards was obliged to make a circuit of the ring to acknowledge the applause.

Pepe Chapi did likewise.

It was now my turn. Fernando motioned to me to slip into the ring with him while Pepe Chapi was still acknowledging the cheers of the crowd. When the cheering subsided and Pepe Chapi had left, Fernando and I slipped in behind the plank shelter. My other two *banderilleros* had taken up their positions in the two plank shelters which were set one on each side of the ring; one to my right and the other to my left. The *areneros* smoothed the sand of the arena.

A heavy and tense silence fell on the crowd as I waited for

93

my bull to be set loose. Fernando whispered last-minute words of advice.

"Now don't forget, *jefe*, wait until I've run the bull at least once on each horn. I'll tell you when to come out," he instructed.

"All right," I replied.

"Just keep calm and you'll be all right. Imagine that you are at a *tienta* and forget about the public."

"O.K.," I murmured. I was beginning to feel scared again and wanted to relieve myself, but knew that this was impossible now.

The president gave the signal and the trumpet shrilled. I watched as the man who was in charge of the bull-pens advanced towards the gate where the bulls came in. ("The gate of the big fear," the bullfighters call it. I now knew why.) He reached the gate, unlatched it and swung it wide open. I tried to penetrate its inky blackness but could see nothing.

A shout went up from the crowd, but it was not to greet the entry of the bull. A little black cat had walked into the ring from the bull-pens and everybody, myself included, burst out laughing. The tension was broken and my confidence was restored.

In came my bull and a cheer broke from the crowd. It was a perfect specimen of a fighting bull: short, stocky and perfectly proportioned, with symmetrically curving horns. It halted a few paces from the gate to the pens and stood still. I could see the hump of the tossing muscle rising on its great neck as it slowly took stock of its surroundings.

The *banderillero* to my left stepped out from behind his shelter and showed himself to the bull. The reaction was immediate. Like a bolt, the bull charged across the ring and as it did so the *banderillero* slipped back to his hiding place. The bull pulled up sharply at the barrier and hooked at the planking with its horns. I could see the chips of wood flying at each blow.

I sensed rather than saw Fernando leave my side, and run

94

out into the ring, calling the bull as he did so. The bull by this time had realised the futility of hooking at the barrier and now stood with its tail swishing, looking for something else to attack. It spotted Fernando and immediately charged towards him. Fernando stood his ground and as the bull arrived, swung the cape out with one hand in a wide sweeping arc. The animal followed the cloth perfectly. "He is good on that horn," I thought to myself.

The bull, furious at not having hit anything solid, turned and came at Fernando again on the other side and once more my *banderillero* swung his cape out in a wide arc and once more the bull followed it perfectly.

He was good on both horns and I realised that Miguel and Adolfo hadn't exaggerated after all. At least not as far as this bull was concerned.

Fernando snatched his cape away from under the bull's nose and left the animal looking bewildered and wondering where its target had disappeared to. I stepped out of my shelter and advanced towards the bull. Fernando grinned at me as he passed. His teeth positively flashed in the sunlight as he did so and I realised for the first time that they were all gold.

"It's an animal in a million, *jefe*," he whispered. "If you don't get yourself awarded an ear with this one, you never will. Just take it calmly."

I opened my cape and profiled to the horns. The bull watched me intently with his black beady eyes. I stepped nearer and shook my cape. The tension and silence in the ring were very noticeable. Not a murmur came from the crowd.

I moved a little nearer and called to the bull, "*Aha torito, toma bonito.*" He started for me. I swung the cape out and keeping my hands low I led him past in a *veronica*. Suddenly the bullring exploded with the shout of "*Olé*" from ten thousand voices.

The bull wheeled and came at me again and I made another

95

veronica, and again ten thousand voices shouted as one man. This indeed was the stimulation I needed. I did a third *veronica* and then a *media veronica* to fix the bull in one place. Turning my back on the bull I faced up to the crowd. The applause was deafening and, as is the custom, I took off my hat to acknowledge it. I then decided to do some *chicuelinas*, passes where the bullfighter pulls the cape back on to himself and spins between the horns as the bull turns on him. I called the bull and executed a *chicuelina* and then, as the bull turned and came at me again, I started another. The next thing I knew I was flying through the air. There was a rapid kaleidoscopic view of sand, faces, and blue sky, and then I was lying on my back in the sand.

As rapidly as possible I rolled over on to my stomach and covered my head with my hands as I had seen other bull-fighters do when tossed. The bull was trampling on me now and any moment I expected to feel the horn thrust into my body. It was not, however, and for a second the trampling stopped. I uncovered my head. In that brief instant I was hit in the mouth by what felt like a sledge-hammer. The impact of the blow rolled me completely over and I felt my mouth fill with blood from a gash the horn had made in my lip and on the inside of my cheek and gum. Luckily I must have had my mouth open, otherwise the horn would have smashed through my teeth.

It had all happened in a split second and now my *banderilleros*, together with Miguel Campos and Pepe Chapi, were around me calling the bull off.

Fernando helped me to my feet and over to the barrier where my swordhandler wiped my mouth and gave me a glass of water so that I could swill out some of the blood. Miguel, my manager, was looking worried.

"You'd better get along to the *enfermeria* and get that fixed, Vicente," he said.

(*Above*) A *derechazo* with a fast-moving bull. (*Photo: Perez-Ponce.*) (*Below*) Terminating a *faena* with a right-handed *pase de pecho*.

(*Above*) A two-handed *pase por alto*, following through. (*Photo: Baker.*) (*Below*) A right-handed *pase por alto*. (*Photo: Perez-Ponce.*)

"*Mierda!* It's nothing," I replied. "Pedro, give me another cape, quickly," I shouted at my swordhandler.

"It was your own fault, *jefe*," said Fernando; "you kept your elbows into your sides and pulled the bull on to yourself. Don't forget he will go where you send him."

I turned away quickly and rudely. I did not want to start having lessons on bullfighting at this stage.

After completing a couple more passes, the trumpet sounded for the *banderillas* to be placed and I retired to the barrier. Pedro handed me a towel to wipe the sweat from my face and I took a swig of water to rinse my mouth. I spat the water into the sand and watched as the globules of liquid turned into dust balls which rolled in all directions from the point of impact. My *banderilleros* made short work of placing the darts, and the trumpet sounded for the last act to begin. Pedro handed me my folded *muleta* and sword, and crossing them I held both in my left hand as I had practised. I then removed my hat and advanced towards the president's box to go through the formality of asking his permission to kill the bull. Stopping before his box I raised my hat towards him and said, "Good afternoon, sir. With your permission?" He smilingly nodded his assent.

At this moment I happened to look down and noticed a bottle-cap lying in the sand. The ring of the bottle had broken off and I could see the circle of glass gleaming inside the metal cap. For some reason it annoyed me and I knew that I would have to remove it from the sand before I began the final act.

Having received the president's permission to go ahead, I walked over to where Mr. Gomez, the British Vice-Consul, was sitting in the front row, to dedicate the bull to him. Mr. Gomez stood up as I arrived before him, and raising my arm holding my hat in his direction I said, "I have the honour to dedicate the death of this bull, the first I shall kill in my life as a professional bullfighter, to you, Mr. Gomez, as representative of my country in La Linea." I then tossed up my hat to him. Catching it, he smiled in acknowledgement and sat down.

Turning to where Fernando was keeping the bull's attention whilst all this was going on I motioned to him to bring the animal to just the other side of the presidential box. I could read the look of mystification on his face as if to say, "It's all right here, why bother to take it over there." But it is a *banderillero's* obligation to obey the *matador* at all times and to take the bull wherever the *matador* chooses to fight it. Fernando obeyed immediately and caped the bull to the position I had indicated. He still looked quizzical as he passed me on his way back to the barrier.

Walking towards the bull I kept glancing down on the ground and then I spotted it again. That offending bottle top. With the point of the sword I flicked the circle of metal under the barrier. Now I could carry on. It never occurred to me that it was a silly thing to worry about, or that the onlookers would wonder what on earth I was doing. It was something that just had to be done.

Waiting until I was about six paces from the bull, I let the *muleta* fall open and spread the cloth over the sword. I would begin with a *pase de la muerte*. The bull watched interestedly, wondering what his new adversary might be. I shook the cloth gently and called to him. He charged and I waited for him with my feet together, firmly planted in the sand. His horns arrived at the cloth of the *muleta*, I raised my hands and he passed underneath, his nearside horn grazing my chest. He went through and quickly turning came at the *muleta* again. I did not move a muscle until he was up to the *muleta*. Again the horn passed a few inches from my body. I repeated this four times and I was conscious of the cries of "*Olé*" from the crowd. The band struck up with a *pasodoble*. I continued with the right hand, then the left, and then went through my repertoire of fancy passes. At one point I stretched out my

98

hand and held the bull's horn to show how close I was fighting. Twice more I was tossed, fortunately without serious consequences, but by this time I was too intoxicated by this new experience to care what happened. All the time I was remembering Pajarero's instructions, like those of an old sweat to a recruit: "If you get your guts ripped out, hold them in with one hand and keep on fighting with the other." That was exaggerating a bit but I knew what he meant by it. The important thing was to keep on fighting.

The time had now come for me to kill. I lined the bull up and making sure that his forefeet were in line, I raised my sword, sighted along the blade, and fell on the bull. The blade of the sword disappeared into the beast's body and only the red hilt showed between its shoulders. It staggered, coughed, and crashed to the sand, dead!

After saluting the president I went over to Mr. Gomez, who returned my hat. The crowd went wild and Beaty grabbed my hand and shook it madly. "You've done it. You've done it, Vicente. It was terrific," he said.

The seats were a mass of white handkerchiefs and I knew that the public were asking the president to award me the ears. My *banderilleros* were standing by the carcase of the bull awaiting the president's signal, and in readiness to cut off what he had decided was to be my award.

Pedro handed me a towel and I wiped my hands and face. "We were good, *jefe*," he said. I smiled at him and his pleasure. It was a triumph for the whole *cuadrilla*.

Suddenly Fernando came up behind me. "Here you are, *jefe*, look what they have given us." Saying this he handed me the two ears and the tail of the bull. I was speechless. This was beyond my wildest expectations.

Taking the ears in one hand and the tail in the other I turned to the president and held the trophies aloft. He nodded his confirmation of the award and I bowed my thanks to him before starting off on a circuit of the ring. The crowd were wild with excitement and standing up in their seats they showered the ring with articles of apparel, flowers, wine-skins and cigars. The latter my *cuadrilla* pocketed, the rest they threw back.

Having once been right the way round the ring, Fernando insisted that I went to the *enfermeria* to have my mouth attended to. This was to be my first but by no means my last journey to a bullring's "hospital". This time I was, at least, able to walk there. The doctor swabbed the lacerated part and strapped it together. I refused to have stitches as I didn't wish the wound to leave a scar. It was a matter of minutes before I returned to the ring; Miguel Campos had just finished killing his second bull and Pepe Chapi was preparing for his.

Pedro, my swordhandler, started to sew up the tears in my breeches. He made a first-class job of them and finished just in time for me to slip into the ring and await my second bull.

Taking my place beside my *banderillero* I watched intently as the door to the bull-pens was swung open. Would my next bull be as good as the first? That would be too much to hope for, I thought. I had already had more luck than I deserved.

"The gate of the big fear" opened to reveal the tunnel from which the bull would be loosed, and almost immediately he burst into the ring. He positively hurtled in and spotting his shadow on the barrier, immediately began to attack it. He did a half-circuit of the ring in this manner, attacking his own shadow with ferocity.

"*Es muy bravo*," said Fernando, "It is very wild."

It looked as if Adolfo and my manager had been right about both bulls after all. Fernando stepped out and ran the bull first on one side then on the other. The animal followed perfectly. Fernando then stopped it about seven yards from where I was standing and without hesitation I stepped out from behind the barrier.

As before, I started with *veronicas*, finishing with a half *veronica*. Again the "*olés*" cracked out like pistol shots from the crowd and I started another series of passes called *gaoneras*, in which the bullfighter holds the cape behind his body. The bull was passing so close that his shoulder bumped my chest each time, and later Pedro showed me the black hairs that he had picked out of the embroidery on the front of my jacket.

The *banderilleros* placed the darts quickly and efficiently and the time came for the last act. This time I decided to dedicate the bull to the crowd.

After receiving the sword and *muleta* from Pedro, I took off my hat and going out to the centre of the ring I held it at arm's length and slowly turning, I described a circle which embraced every part of the public in the bullring. This signified that everyone present was included in the dedication. They were appreciative of this gesture and let me know it by their applause.

My *faena* this time followed closely on the pattern of the previous one and culminated in a single sword thrust. The reaction of the audience was as before and again I was awarded the ears and the tail of the bull.

Whilst I was making the circuit of the ring several enthusiasts climbed down on to the sand and lifted me on their shoulders and carried me round and round the ring to the accompaniment of wild cheers. "This is indeed an honour", I thought; but it was not finished. They carried me out into the street and down towards the *Calle Real*. All the way, people who had not been to the fight came out on to their balconies and cheered loudly. Down the *Calle Real* we went and men sitting in the bars there came out and gave me glasses of wine. Round and round the streets they carried me and so great was my elation that I didn't give a thought to my uncomfortable, even perilous, position. Still the people kept cheering and pressing drinks on me, and it was some time before I could persuade my enthusiastic bearers to carry me back to my room.

The house in which I was living stood in a square which was now packed with people. The noise from their acclamation was terrific and my manager made me go out on to the balcony to acknowledge them. I felt like royalty.

After two or three appearances on the balcony I told Pedro to close the shutters. I was worn out and could hardly stand. Pedro helped me to undress and after taking a shower bath I lay on the bed.

Until then I hadn't realised just how tired I was. The nervous exhaustion that always follows a bullfight hit me and I fell into a sound sleep. However, I wasn't allowed to rest for long. My manager came into the room and waking me told me that his father's bar was full of people who were wanting to congratulate me and that I must go there. The bar was packed, and there followed a mad evening of drinking, hand-shaking and autograph-signing.

Time passed quickly and it was ten o'clock when Miguel took me into the parlour to listen to the bullfight reports on the radio. They gave my appearance precedence over all the other bullfights that had taken place in Spain that day, and it was then that I fully appreciated the extent of my achievements. The hardships I had suffered had been worthwhile. Bullfighting was my life.

7

MY body ached and throbbed all over and my mouth was swollen and painful when I awoke the next morning. Climbing carefully out of bed I removed my pyjama trousers to inspect my legs and found that my thighs were covered in angry red horn burns that now seared painfully. In my medical kit was a bottle of alcohol and pouring a little into my cupped hand I applied it to the damaged skin. The first stinging shock nearly made me jump through the ceiling but shortly afterwards came soothing relief. Slowly and not without a good deal of discomfort I dressed and made my way to my manager's house trying not to limp although I really felt like crawling on all fours. Every muscle in my body ached. Until then I had never realised just how many muscles the human body contained.

I entered Miguel's house just as he was sitting down to breakfast with his family. He invited me to join them. I hadn't eaten at all the previous day and the hot rolls and coffee tasted better than anything I had eaten for a long time.

Miguel showed me the reports of the fight in the morning papers. The critics were enthusiastic.

"It seems to have created quite a stir," I said.

"It has," agreed my manager, "but don't start thinking that you can relax now. You have only just begun."

"When do you think I shall be able to fight again?" I asked.

"Not just yet," said Miguel. "You must practise a lot more. You still have a lot to learn. You were very lucky yesterday, the bulls were perfect, they both ran on rails. You won't always get animals like those."

I was impatient now to have another fight and the thought of having to go through a lot more training without actually fighting real bulls didn't appeal to me.

"When we have finished breakfast we will go to see Adolfo," said Miguel. "He will tell you the same as I have. It's got to be practice, practice, practice from now onwards."

"Not today at least," I complained; "I can hardly walk, let alone run around the bullring."

"All right," Miguel assented. "Hurry up and finish and we will go to the Vice-Consulate."

Adolfo Beaty clapped me on the back when we arrived at his office. "*Que hay*, Vicente? You were fine yesterday. You have created an unprecedented point of discussion. All Spain is talking about your debut."

"Vicente seems to think that all he has to do now is to wait for more contracts to come in," said Miguel.

"Oh no, you've everything to learn," said Adolfo turning to me. "As a matter of fact, Juan Belmonte saw you fight yesterday and he says exactly the same as everyone else. You have the basic qualities to be a good bullfighter but are very, very green. He has invited you to go out to his ranch on Thursday and says that you can stay with him for ten days. Each day he will let you fight ten cows and he himself will give you lessons."

It had long been my ambition to meet the famous Belmonte and I could hardly believe my ears when Adolfo told me this news. That the old *maestro* himself was to give me lessons was unbelievable.

"That's wonderful," I exclaimed, "but why should he take an interest in me?"

"I don't know," replied Adolfo. "His brothers Pepe and Manolo have an interest in the bullring here, together with my father and myself, so maybe that has something to do with it. Anyway, whatever the reason, you are very lucky to receive this invitation."

I realised that I was being offered an opportunity that any other young bullfighter in my position would have gone to great lengths to obtain. I would take full advantage of it.

There were still two days before I was due at the Belmonte ranch and I used these to get in as much practice as possible. Down to the bullring I went to spend long sessions shadow-bullfighting, concentrating on what I had been told were my weakest points.

By Wednesday evening I was very tired and glad to get to bed early. I am not prone to, nor a believer in, dreams but that night I had the most vivid one I had ever experienced. I saw myself at the Belmonte ranch with the *tienta* in progress. The little ring was unlike any I had previously seen. Adjoining the ranch-house it was overlooked by a balcony which gave out from the main lounge. People were seated on this balcony watching me as I fought a cow, when suddenly I saw myself being held by one of the onlookers and heard Belmonte saying, "He has been gored."

When I awoke I was too excited and too busy packing to give my dream a second thought. At ten o'clock Adolfo called for Miguel and myself in his car. I was wearing my country suit, tight trousers and bolero jacket—similar to those worn by Spanish dancers—which bullfighters always wear at *tientas*.

Belmonte's ranch was situated in a town called Utrera on the road between Jerez and Sevilla and it had been arranged that we should stop in Jerez and lunch with Pepe Belmonte, Juan's younger brother, who had also been a *matador* and was now impresario of several bullrings in Andalucia.

I had never been to Jerez before and looked forward eagerly to the brief visit, especially as we were to visit the famous sherry *bodegas*.

After leaving Algeciras the road climbed steadily, hugging the coast as far as Tarifa. The view across the stráits was breathtaking and Ceuta was plainly visible, shimmering white in the distance, bounded by the hills of Morocco. Turning inland from Tarifa we continued climbing as far as Chiclana, where we stopped for a glass of wine, and for the first time I tasted *bocas de la isla*, deliciously succulent crab claws. I asked Adolfo what happened to the rest of the crab and was told that the fishermen just pull off the claws and then throw the crabs back into the sea to grow more.

Passing over the salt flats of Puerta de Santa Maria, we saw storks standing like white sentries guarding the rock-hard pyramids of glaring white salt. Soon we were in Jerez and Adolfo pulled up outside the hotel Los Cisnes. We were sipping a drink when Pepe Belmonte arrived. After we had been introduced he explained that the *tienta* was scheduled to start earlier than had been expected and therefore there would not be enough time for our visit to the *bodegas* after all. This was a disappointment. However, Pepe promised to take me some other time. We ate a hurried lunch and continued the journey to the ranch.

We passed from the vineyards of Jerez to the olive groves that lined the road to Utrera. Suddenly Adolfo swung the car off to the right between two stone pillars that bore the double "J" brand of Juan Belmonte's herd. This brand incorporates the first initial of Juan Belmonte and that of Julia, his wife.

Following the track up to the house, Adolfo stopped the car before a beautiful glass and wrought-iron door which stood half open. We had scarcely alighted when our host, Juan Belmonte, came down the steps that led from the front door and welcomed us. We followed him into the house which was in the style of the other Andalucian ranch-houses that I had visited, with spacious, airy rooms. If anything, Belmonte's place was more modernly furnished than the others. He showed us into the lounge and on entering I had a feeling that I had been there before; then my mind flashed back to my dream of the previous night. I took stock of my surroundings. On one wall hung a portrait of Belmonte dressed in his bullfighting costume, painted by the famous Spanish artist, Zuluaga. At the end of the lounge I noticed a large french-window which I could see gave on to a balcony. Not able to contain my curiosity I walked over to find out whether the balcony overlooked the practice ring. It did. It was exactly as I had seen it in my dream. Belmonte came over to my side and enquired whether I liked the house. I told him that it was beautiful, as indeed it was. He asked if I would like to see the rest of it, and I eagerly said I would. Having shown me round the inside of the house, my host led the way to an outside room that contained the equipment necessary for a ranch of this description. The walls were lined with lances and in one corner hung several pairs of chaps of intricately tooled leather. A group of guests stood at the far end of the room reading a faded bullfight poster announcing one of Belmonte's earliest fights. The *ex-torero* took me over to the group and immediately I recognised several faces from my dream. The feeling that it had all happened before grew stronger and stronger and I became certain that some misfortune was impending. Strangely enough, this didn't bother me. It seemed too late to be afraid of anything that might occur. I would have to wait and see what the very near future held.

Belmonte announced that it was time for us to go down into the ring as the *vaqueros* had the cows penned, ready for us to begin. The only other bullfighter present was Belmonte's son, Juanito. Together we took our places and the *tienta* commenced. As this *tienta* was being held for my benefit, I was to fight all ten cows and not alternate with Juanito, who was my senior as a *matador*. The cows were very fast, much faster than any I had previously encountered, and this fact, combined with the feeling of impending disaster, unsettled me. I found myself unable to reproduce anything like my best form.

It was just after the third cow had entered the ring that I realised I was missing an opportunity of a lifetime. Here I was, being given a chance to prove myself before one of the divinities of the *taurine* world, and doing absolutely nothing about it. With great determination I faced the cow after receiving Belmonte's instructions to take her with the *muleta*. I went through everything I knew but I was aware that there was still something lacking in my performance. As I prepared to start another series of left-handed passes, Belmonte called to me to let the animal go, saying that she had been fought for too long and was fast learning the difference between my body and the *muleta*. Not heeding his warning I started another *faena*. My confidence had returned and now I would show what I was capable of. The first pass went according to plan, but between that and the second the inevitable happened and the cow chopped in, burying her horn in my left groin. I felt the horn enter my leg and grabbed its base with both hands, trying desperately to reach the ground with my feet. Then, as she started to toss, I spun head downward, falling heavily on the earth. Willing hands helped me to my feet and I distinctly remember hearing Belmonte say "*Tiene una cornada*"—He's been gored.

Someone ripped open the hole in my trousers to examine the wound, and looking down I saw fine jets of blood spurting with each pulse beat. I had never before bled in this manner and it seemed unreal and nothing to do with me. They carried me into the house and laid me down in the bathroom. It was miraculously lucky that one of the guests had several packets of penicillin with him. At that time this antibiotic was very difficult to obtain in Spain but there was a considerable traffic in it from Gibraltar. After packing the wound with penicillin and plugging the mouth of it with gauze, my manager firmly bandaged the dressing and enquired.

"How does that feel, Vicente?"

"It doesn't hurt at all," I replied truthfully. Apart from a peculiar numbness inside my leg, I felt no pain.

"You'd better sit up on the balcony with Belmonte until we are ready to take you to the hospital," he advised.

Leaning on his shoulder, I walked back to the *tienta* ring where Belmonte came forward and asked how I was. I told him the same as I had told Miguel, that apart from the numbness I felt all right.

"If you think you can make it, go down into the ring and try a few more passes. There is a new cow being let in now. Juanito will help you," said Belmonte. "It's like an airman crashing. If he can, the best thing to do is to take up another 'plane immediately, to restore his confidence."

Taking his advice, I walked somewhat unsteadily and not without apprehension down to the ring and taking the *muleta* from Juanito I made a few more passes. They were nothing stylish but they did the trick. By now my leg began to stiffen and the numbness was giving way to pain so I hobbled back to the balcony.

"Adolfo is getting the car," said Miguel. "We'll see how you feel when we get to Jerez. We can either leave you there or carry on to La Linea."

"I think I would rather go back to La Linea if possible," I replied.

"Is it beginning to hurt much?" Belmonte asked me.

"It is now," I confessed.

"Where? Under the hip?" he enquired.

"Yes, and further down inside my thigh," I told him.

"Probably two trajectories. I thought so by the way you turned on the horn," he said, with the air of one who had received so many horn wounds that he was an authority on the subject.

Adolfo arrived and announced that all was ready for the drive back and with Miguel's help he carried me down to the car. Then began a journey that I shall never forget.

With every mile the stiffness in my leg increased and the pain became agony. It was a bumpy road we travelled and every bump sent a shock of searing pain through my groin. Adolfo slowed the car to a crawl and at this pace we crept forward to Jerez. On arriving in the town, Miguel, who was in a state of panic by now, insisted that I should go to hospital there, but I didn't relish the idea of being left in a place where I knew nobody and after all, having come so far it would be worthwhile continuing the journey to La Linea. On we pressed. The pain and the fact that I was chain-smoking made me feel sick and Adolfo had to keep stopping the car for me. Eventually, after what seemed an eternity, we arrived in La Linea at 1 a.m.

Pulling up in front of the doctor's house, Miguel and Adolfo carried me inside and put me on the inspection table. The doctor came in wearing pyjamas and looking very sleepy. He undid the bandage, pulled out the gauze plug and rammed his finger into the hole. This was unbearable and without a second thought I sat up and punched him on the jaw, swearing at him in English. He was taken aback, but not so much as I when he said to me in English that he didn't mind in the least if I hit him but he was very upset that I should revile him as I did. He explained that it was necessary to inspect the wound in this way so as to ascertain the amount of damage done by the horn. Making Adolfo and Miguel hold me down on the table he again pushed his finger inside the wound and probed around. Having satisfied himself as to the extent of the injury he gave me two injections, one anti-gangrene and the other anti-tetanus. He then told Miguel and Adolfo to take me along to the hospital, saying that he would operate first thing in the morning.

The night was interminable and it was a relief to hear that the doctor was waiting. I donned an operating gown and hobbled to the operating theatre between two male nurses. They explained that the trolley they usually employed was out of action.

Inside the theatre the capped and gowned surgeon and anaesthetist stood waiting. I was helped on to the operating table and the anaesthetist placed the rubber cap over my mouth and nose. Following his instructions I breathed deeply, inhaling the sickly anaesthetic, and soon began to lapse into the unconsciousness which I craved to bring me relief from the agony I was suffering. In a matter of seconds my head began to clear and I realised with a start that no anaesthetic was coming through the machine. I tried desperately to attract attention by shaking my head but it was firmly held between the hands of one of the male nurses. I struggled harder and received what I supposed to be a calmative punch on the side of my head. Then, realising that all was not well, he removed the mask from my face, unscrewed a nozzle from the machine, placed it to his lips, blew through it, replaced it and jammed the mask none too gently over my mouth and nose. This unorthodox method of repair was effective and soon I was lost in oblivion.

The following three hours were completely lost to me. The surgeon worked with skill and efficacy. What these small town surgeons lack in equipment they more than make up for in dexterity and dedication to their work.

Regaining consciousness later, my first thoughts were about what had passed, the goring and the operation. I could feel no pain and found it difficult to believe that it had ever existed. Drowsily I opened my eyes. Immediately I saw a nun, the Mother Superior, holding a crucifix over me, and several serious-looking people grouped around the bed. I decided there and then that I was dying and being given the last Sacraments. My thoughts flew to my family. I had cabled them after my fight and they had written saying they were coming out to see me for a short holiday. Now they would arrive too late; I would be dead. Again I lapsed into unconsciousness.

It may have been only a few minutes later—I had no notion of time—when I recovered my senses. The sombre group still stood around the bed and nobody spoke a word. I really am dead, I thought, so there must be a life hereafter. I can see these people around me, so my spirit must be alive. Any minute I expected it to leave my body and pass to the unknown beyond. Then my manager spoke.

"How do you feel, Vicente?" he enquired anxiously.

He was looking at me and talking to me. I couldn't have left this world after all. My first feeling was one of intense disappointment. Thinking I had experienced death and finding it was nothing to be feared, I now realised that I had been mistaken and that one day I would have to go through it again. Closing my eyes, I fell into an exhausted sleep.

The following morning my first visitors arrived at 8 a.m. and the last left seventeen and a half hours later at 1.30 a.m. Apart from when I asked for the room to be cleared so that I might answer the calls of nature, I wasn't left alone all day. Miguel arrived with newspaper cuttings bearing accounts of the accident. "*El Ingles* receives his baptism of blood," they said. I realised that the British press would probably pick up the story and tell my parents, so I asked Miguel to send a cable to my home explaining that the whole thing was just a publicity stunt. However, my parents were not to be deceived and that evening there came a telephone call from my father. As he could speak no Spanish and no one in the hospital could speak any English, he was unable to get any information about my condition, which caused him to worry even more.

The next day the stream of visitors continued, as in fact it did until I was finally discharged from hospital. Literally hundreds of people came, bearing gifts of flowers, cakes, cigarettes and cigars. The latter were quickly pocketed by my manager. People I had never met crowded into my room anxiously enquiring how I felt and if there was anything that I needed. Their kindness was overwhelming.

With the third day started the course of treatment which I came to dread. It was far more painful than the actual goring. Each morning the male nurse would unplug from the wound the yards of gauze with which it was packed. This, I learned, was to facilitate drainage. He would explore its nethermost parts with a steel probe to ascertain its satisfactory progress, then swab and repack it. The cure was far worse than the cause and my manager used to hold a twisted towel for me to bite on, the pain was so severe.

I had been in hospital about ten days, when I received a letter from my parents telling me that they were due to arrive in Gibraltar by air in two days' time. Hospital visits are depressing affairs at the best of times and I could imagine what my parents' feelings would be, arriving in a strange country and spending most of their time by a hospital bed, so I asked the doctor if I might be moved to a nearby hotel. He agreed to the idea and immediately a suite was arranged for me with the adjoining one reserved for my parents.

When they arrived at the hotel they were both relieved to find me looking so well. My father took over the job of entertaining the visitors who still kept up a steady flow all day and every day. On one occasion the local football team together with their opponents all piled into my room. Altogether there were about thirty people in the sitting-room, drinking sherry and talking at the tops of their voices. It was a strange atmosphere for an invalid.

The speed at which horn wounds heal is incredible and I

have heard it suggested that the horn itself possesses some curative property. It is well known that witch doctors use powdered horn as a medicine and also as an aphrodisiac. I have known bullfighters receive terrible wounds and be at death's door, yet once past the danger point they seem to make remarkable recoveries and in no time are back in the ring again.

On the fifteenth day I had the stitches removed and received the pleasing news that I would be able to get up the following day for a little while. Miguel had a pair of crutches made for me and I looked forward to getting out of bed again. I was tired of the inactivity and anxious to get my leg strong again.

All would have gone well but that night I developed tetanus. I awoke in the middle of the night with a terrific cramping pain in my arms and legs. I had a raging thirst and tried to sit up to reach the bottle of mineral water that was on the bedside table. I found that I couldn't move and endeavoured to shout to my parents, but this was of no avail as my teeth were tightly clamped together. As I became more fully awake, so I became more conscious of the pain in my limbs and jaw. Helpless and in burning agony I had to lie the rest of the night looking longingly at the tantalising bottle.

In the morning, my mother came to see me and guessed immediately what had happened. I indicated how badly I needed a drink, so pouring the tea from the teapot and refilling it with water, she was able in this manner to drip the liquid between my lips.

The doctor called to see me and left strict instructions that there were to be no visitors. During the course of the day he gave me several injections and last thing at night administered a barbiturate to ensure that I would sleep. By the evening my arms had drawn up across my chest and my hands had clenched and turned inwards. My legs too were drawn up and my toes clenched. The pain was agonising and in no way could I relieve it; movement was impossible.

The drugs took effect and I fell into a heavy slumber. My temperature had risen to 106° F and I sweated profusely. In the morning my mattress had to be changed as it was completely saturated in perspiration. The whole time my mother remained at my bedside, continually giving me sips of water through the teapot spout. The doctor came and administered more drugs which sent me almost immediately into a comatose sleep. He told my mother that either I would die under coma or awake to find the paralysis broken. There was nothing more he could do.

After forty-eight hours of unconsciousness, I awoke and found that the pain had eased considerably. I was still sweating heavily and again the mattress had to be changed, but I was on the mend. Twenty-four hours later I felt fighting fit and when no one was around I carefully climbed out of bed, put on my dressing gown and with the aid of the crutches managed to hobble into the sitting-room. My parents came in to find me sitting in an armchair sipping sherry.

A few days later I took my parents over to Gibraltar for their first sight-seeing visit there, but everywhere we went we were followed by a mob of fans. They even poured into the shops after us and in one place where we wished to buy some shirt silk the proprietor had to lock the doors and call the police to deal with the crowd. My parents were bewildered by it all.

As soon as my leg was strong enough for me to walk around with just one stick, I took my mother and father on a tour of Andalucia. We left La Linea for Malaga and then went on to Granada. From Granada we moved to Ronda and then to Sevilla. Everywhere we went I was recognised and crowds gathered with amazing speed. It was very flattering but afforded us little privacy.

Miguel met us in Sevilla with the news that Belmonte had invited us to go to his ranch so that I might fight a few cows for the benefit of my parents, who were resolute in their decision not to watch me fight in public.

Pepe Belmonte met us in Jerez at the hotel "Los Cisnes" where we were staying. He had arranged for us to visit the sherry *bodegas* of Gonzalez Byass, and led the way through blazing sunshine to the cool buildings that comprised the *bodega*. We were shown all round the place and saw every stage of the industry from grape juice to fermented wine and distilled brandy. After sampling most of the barrels we finished up in what is called the hall of fame. Here were stacked three-hundred-litre barrels, rack upon rack, and most of them were autographed by well-known people. Our guide, one of the young Gonzalezes, invited me to sign a barrel, saying that the contents were mine and for the use of any friends I might care to invite to the *bodega* at any time.

We were given a glass of wonderful 140-year-old sherry known as "Methusela". By this time we were all feeling the effects of sampling so much liquor and it was time for the *pièce de résistance*.

An old chap looked after the *bodegas*—a sort of privileged watchman who had been with the company for over fifty years and had once been pensioned off suffering with diabetes. In gratitude for his long years of service he had been sent out to the country and given the best medical attention, but he had missed his work and throwing away his insulin had returned to die in the atmosphere that he loved. That had all been about fifteen years previously and he still showed no signs of leaving this world. His sole job now was to walk around and generally keep an eye on things. For his amusement he had tamed the mice in the place and was always allowed to show off his pets when visitors were well "conditioned".

Telling us to keep quiet, he went over to one of the barrels and turned the tap to allow a thin flow of wine to pour to the ground. In no time at all, mice began to appear from all directions and drink from the puddle that had formed. They were soon quite drunk and I couldn't help wondering whether alcoholics in the mouse world see pink humans when they get D.T.s! The old chap had fixed up little rope ladders and at the tops of these he placed small pieces of food. The mice kept trying to climb but before they got half-way up they would fall drunkenly to the ground. We never found out whether any of them actually reached the top for Pepe Belmonte told us that it was time to go back to the hotel.

After lunch the hired car that Pepe had ordered for us arrived and we started for Utrera. We made good progress until about fifteen miles from Belmonte's place, when suddenly the car began to lurch and bump all over the road as if it had a puncture. The driver pulled up and we all piled out to discover the cause of this erratic behaviour. Going round to the back of the car we saw that the offside rear wheel stood out about three inches from the body. Unlike the rest of us, the driver didn't appear to be over-concerned about this and immediately set to work with a hammer to rectify matters. Evidently the single nut which held the wheel in position had stripped its thread, so he banged the wheel back, slipped the nut over the spindle and, to hold it in place, hammered a lead washer into the thread of the spindle. We finished our journey to the ranch and later returned to Jerez—a distance of some sixty miles or more—thanks to this effective though precarious method of repair.

I fought about half a dozen cows that afternoon and tried to show my parents that bullfighting was not as dangerous as they would believe. However, my mother was not to be convinced and didn't enjoy it at all. She sat on the edge of her chair and jumped every time the animals charged. My father thought it was great and when the last cow was let into the ring, asked if he might try his hand at it. He came down into the ring and, with Belmonte, made a pass called *el alimon* in which two people advance towards the animal each holding a corner of the cape which is raised as the beast charges, thus leading it between two bodies.

The cow charged and with Belmonte my father executed the pass successfully. Father was excited and wanted to try again, this time alone. He told Belmonte, who dubiously agreed. Miguel was asked to act as photographer. The cow charged straight at my father and tossed him. He escaped with only a few bruises and was as pleased as punch. Not only would he be able to tell his friends in Hatton Garden that he had done some bullfighting during his holiday, but also that he had actually been tossed and had the photograph to prove it. Unfortunately, however, in the excitement Miguel had forgotten to press the shutter button.

After an excellent dinner, we returned to La Linea. My parents were due to leave for London in a week's time and I'd persuaded them to take the 'plane from Madrid instead of Gibraltar so that they might have a few days in that wonderful capital. We left the next day on the express.

One of the first things I did after our arrival in Madrid was to take them along to a bullfighters' outfitters and order a suit. I reminded my father of the rash promise he made before I left London. He had said that if ever I became a bullfighter he would buy me my first costume. He paid up like the sportsman he was, even though it set him back £70. My mother chose the colour, a light bottle-green. The tailor showed us a suit in the same colour that had just been completed. It was magnificent and as he turned the jacket in the sunlight the gold embroidery scintillated like a million golden fireflies. The Spanish name for the costume, *traje de luces*, or suit of lights, could not be more apt.

All the time my parents were in Spain they tried desperately to dissuade me from continuing my career in the bullring but I remained adamant. During the few days we spent together in Madrid they redoubled their efforts to persuade me to return to London with them and were terribly disappointed when they had to leave on the 'plane alone.

8

WHILST I was in Madrid I met Vicente Escribano
again, who told me of the difficulty he was having in
finding himself a manager and that there was very
little prospect of his getting any contracts. I invited him to
return to La Linea with me, saying that I was sure that Miguel
could do something for him. I told him that I would make it
a condition in my contracts that he was to appear on the same
bill.

My leg was rapidly getting back to normal and on returning
to La Linea Vicente Escribano and I trained hard together.
Then came the day when I received an invitation from Fernando Vazquez—the bull-breeder who had asked me to my
second *tienta*—to stay on his ranch for as long as I wished.
There would be plenty of horse riding, shooting and most
important of all, daily practice with the cows. I lost no time
in getting there.

The life I led out on the ranch was ideal. Most of the day
was spent riding with the *vaqueros*, herding the bulls; then in
the late afternoon I would fight two or three cows and afterwards go shooting. Luckily there were plenty of rabbits,
partridges, pigeons and larger game too (the cork forests
abounded with wild boar and deer), as we relied for meat
entirely on what we bagged.

With the numerous opportunities I had of fighting live
animals, my style and technique rapidly improved and I found
that I was being tossed less often. Miguel came out to the
ranch and told me that he had signed a contract for Vicente

Escribano and me to appear in Algeciras. The bulls were to be from the Vazquez ranch.

It was about a week before the fight that I received a letter from a girl I had known for some years in England—her name was Jacqueline Hunwick but I knew her as Jill. Her parents owned a confectioner's shop in Ilford where I had lived for some time. In her letter she said that she and her young brother, Peter, were coming out to Spain for a holiday to see me, and would be arriving in Algeciras on the morning of the Sunday I was due to fight. I was looking forward to her visit as I was greatly needing some female companionship. The one and only Spanish custom that I couldn't agree with was the congregation of the sexes.

On the morning of the fight I arrived in Algeciras about 10 a.m. The train on which Jill was to arrive was due at 11 a.m., so I had an hour in which to get my stuff unpacked and go to Mass. As on the morning of my previous fight, Pedro laid out my costume and then accompanied me to church. The new gold and green suit looked so beautiful that I was impatient to put it on and leave for the bullring.

After Mass, Pedro accompanied me to the station to await the train. It was half an hour late but the delay was forgotten when I saw the tall, slender form of Jill who looked more attractive than ever. She told me the journey had upset her but after we had installed her luggage at the hotel I managed to persuade her to come to the bullring with me and see the bulls sorted. Her brother, a likeable schoolboy who kept up a ceaseless flow of inane conversation, came with us.

I liked the look of the two bulls that I drew. The first was a small black one and the other, the largest of the six, was black and white, and turned out to be one of the best bulls that I ever fought.

Immediately the *sorteo* was over and the animals penned ready for the afternoon, I took Jill back to the hotel to lie down. After seeing her safely settled in bed I told her brother to call me if anything were needed, then went to my room to rest until it was time to leave for the ring.

This time my fears were much less than on the previous occasion and it was not until I was actually in the ring awaiting the signal to make the parade that I felt any real pangs. That is always a bad moment and the more one fights and the more one sees, the more bowel-twisting it becomes.

Jill had decided not to come to the fight and her brother said that he would stay and look after her. I said goodbye and went to join my *cuadrilla* in the car. Pedro had to make the journey to the bullring on the running-board as there was no room for him inside.

The fight went off very well. My first bull, the little black one, was bad and I couldn't manage to do anything outstanding with him but I killed with one thrust and was awarded an ear. The second bull, the black and white one, was magnificent. He had a broad forehead covered in a mass of white curly hair. If ever a bull had a kind face, this one had. He was very brave and attacked repeatedly and frankly, enabling me to do *faena* after *faena*. Again I killed with the first swordthrust and after being awarded the two ears and the tail by the president, was carried back to the hotel shoulder high.

Jill was still feeling ill when I arrived back at the hotel and as soon as Pedro had helped me out of my sweat-saturated clothes I sent him off for a doctor. The doctor gave her a tonic and came in to chat with me whilst I was still under the shower. He said that with rest she would be all right in the morning. She was sleeping when I went to her room so with Pedro I left to meet my *cuadrilla*. We had arranged to have a drink after the fight and I was anxious to hear their opinion of the afternoon's performance.

Entering the *Club Nautico* we made for the table where the *cuadrilla* were sitting drinking. As we approached, they stood up and we exchanged congratulations as is customary between *matadores* and their teams. The congratulations are on coming through the fight safely, not on the performance.

"Well, *jefe*," said Fernando, after Pedro and I had sat down and ordered drinks, "what did you think of this afternoon's job?"

"I was going to ask you the same thing, Fernando," I said. "For myself I was pleased but I want to hear your opinion. You were able to see my work in its proper perspective. Being in close contact with the bull all the time makes it difficult to analyse one's performance; that's why I want your opinion. We are a team and we are all in this together so don't be afraid to criticise."

"Quite honestly, *jefe*," replied Fernando, "you were much better than in your first fight. You're beginning to look more at home in the ring and moving like a *torero*. Most important, you are beginning to loosen up and put more feeling into your work. Last time you fought as an Englishman, cold and aloof, without allowing yourself to be in harmony with the bull. Today anybody would have thought you a Spaniard, and if you want to be a good bullfighter that is how you must be. It is impossible to fight bulls and to think in English, just as it would be impossible for a Spaniard to play cricket and think in Spanish. It is a question of *temperamento*."

My mind flashed back to my travelling companion on that first train journey from Madrid to Algeciras when I arrived in Spain, and to the words of Señor Vallejo: "The English have not the right *temperamento*."

"It's good to hear that Fernando," I told my *banderillero*.

Miguel came in and joined us at the table. I hadn't seen him after the fight as he had gone to collect the money from the promoter. He more or less repeated what Fernando had said and then, after asking Pedro for the accounts, he paid the *cuadrilla*. With money in our pockets we all started ordering drinks and were soon quite merry. Suddenly I remembered that I hadn't seen Escribano since leaving the bullring.

"Have you seen Vicente Escribano?" I asked Miguel.

"No. He's probably ashamed to show his face," my manager replied. "That first bull of his was perfect and he was terrified of getting within a yard of it. I thought you said he was good."

"I'd never seen him fight except at the *tientas* and he gave me the impression that he knew his stuff," I replied. I was annoyed with Vicente for letting me down after paying his fare and hotel bills and recommending him to Miguel.

"He knows his stuff all right," said Miguel furiously, "but he is too afraid to look at the bulls. I bet he is back at the hotel right now, washing out his underpants."

I decided to change the subject.

"How about having something to eat?" I suggested.

"Come on then. Let's go now," said Miguel. "Pompof and Thedy, the clowns, are appearing here tonight and have invited us all to go along to the circus."

The circus was good. I have never failed to be thrilled by the blaze of lights and the noise that are so much a part of the sawdust ring. Pompof and Thedy gave a wonderful performance of clowning. They finished their act by cracking jokes about me and, pointing us out in the audience, had me spotlighted, which I found extremely embarrassing.

The clowns joined us after the show and we all went to a nearby café for a nightcap. The *cuadrilla* had a couple of drinks, then left for their respective homes. Miguel and I were just preparing to leave when in walked Juan Gallardo the bull-breeder. After consuming a good few more brandies, someone suggested that we should go to one of the *ventas*—roadside cafés—where one can sing and dance *flamenco* all night.

On entering the *venta*, the first person we saw was Vicente Escribano, who was very drunk and dancing with a trollop.

Spotting our arrival, he immediately dropped the girl and came over to join us.

Juan Gallardo suggested that we should take a private room and engage a guitarist. We agreed enthusiastically and the rest of the night was spent in singing and dancing. I was gradually picking up the rhythm of the various types of song and learning the complicated handclap accompaniment.

It was 8 a.m. when I arrived back at the hotel to find Jill furious that I should have stayed out all night. I explained that she had been asleep when I left, and anyway, I asked, what was it to her how I spent my nights? From her reply I gathered she considered that we were engaged. Some years previously, when we were much younger, I had suggested the same thing to her but she had demurred, saying that she was going to be a schoolteacher and had no intention ever of marrying. However, from then onwards, I introduced her as my fiancée and all my friends thought it rather strange that I hadn't mentioned her before.

Vicente Escribano and I breakfasted and then took Jill and her brother Peter over to La Linea by car. Wherever we went people stared in wonderment at Peter's hair. It was flaming red and an amazing sight for a Spaniard to behold.

On Wednesday evening I returned to the ranch to get into training for a fight which was to be held in La Linea the following Sunday, in honour of the local football team who had just been moved up a division. Jill drove out to the ranch with me and then returned to La Linea with Miguel. Poor Miguel didn't fancy the idea of driving back with her alone as he had been engaged to be married for eight years and he thought his fiancée might be jealous if she knew that he had been alone in the car with Jill. However, they managed to arrive in La Linea unnoticed and Miguel was saved an embarrassing situation.

I missed Jill while I was on the ranch. I would have liked

to have had her there with me but Fernando Vazquez's mother lived in the house and had rather strict views on such things. Even Miguel was horrified when I suggested this to him.

"You might just as well stay in La Linea until the fight," he said.

"But Jill would love it on the ranch," I argued.

"I daresay she would but remember you are a *torero* now and have a responsibility to your public, Vicente," he answered.

I couldn't figure this out.

It was not until early Sunday morning that I returned to La Linea. Vicente Escribano was appearing with me and a nephew of Manolete, a boy called Rafael Sanchez Saco, was making his debut. Together with Vicente I was to go down to have a look at the bulls, but at the last minute Jill decided to come with us and eventually when we arrived at the bull-ring, the animals had already been sorted and penned. It was while we were there that I heard for the first time that arrangements had been made for Jill to head the parade across the ring on horseback and ask for the key to the bull-pens—a custom practised in a lot of bullrings on special occasions. I was furious when I heard about this and told Adolfo Beaty that unless he cancelled the idea I would not honour my contract. I had never seen Jill on a horse and didn't even know if she knew how to ride. The horses often shy at the noise of the spectators and I didn't fancy the idea of her being thrown in the middle of the bullring.

Miguel managed to get a couple of ringside seats for Jill and her brother and I promised to hand her up my dress cape. I also decided to dedicate one of the bulls to her but didn't tell her so.

The bulls turned out to be the worst that I had yet come up against. My first animal, roan-coloured and ugly in shape, would not attack at all and after chasing him all over the ring I managed to kill him cleanly. I was annoyed because I had particularly wanted to put up a good show in front of Jill. The public applauded the kill and I was obliged to make a circuit of the ring to acknowledge their acclamations, but they booed the bull.

The second animal turned out to be very much better and I contrived to do a varied *faena*, finally killing it in front of where Jill was sitting. The public went wild. They loved the romantic idea of my dedicating a bull to my fiancée, especially as I was tossed just in front of her. I was given both the ears and chaired from the ring.

Two days later I was due to return to the ranch and after lunch Fernando Vazquez came into town to pick me up in his car. Peter was to come with us. We stopped at a *venta* a few miles before reaching the ranch and had some wine. After having several "last ones for the road" we eventually drove back to La Linea. Miguel was furious when he saw me back there as I was due to appear in Grazalema the following weekend. It was the annual fair and I had been contracted to fight on three consecutive days. Despite my manager's opposition I stayed in town until we left for Grazalema.

On the Friday, I decided to take Jill and Peter with me so that once the fights were over we could go on to Ronda for a few days. We took the train from Algeciras, leaving it at Cortes to pile into the most ancient car it has ever been my misfortune to ride in. After a seemingly endless journey over a tortuous mountain road, we arrived in Grazalema and were deposited in front of its one and only boarding-house. Our rooms, although on the same floor, were all at different levels and angles. Below us were the stables and the aroma was "farmyard" to say the least.

The first fight was scheduled to take place at four-thirty the next day and as I was eager to take a look at the bullring we made it our first visit. It was a weird affair constructed entirely of wood and not very strong wood at that. The bulls arrived that evening, being driven in a herd through the streets to the corrals. They were minute and I was relieved; any decent-sized bull would have torn that bullring to match-wood.

The streets of Grazalema were too narrow and uneven for a car to be of any use and this was the first and only time that the *cuadrilla* and I had to walk to the bullring. At 4 p.m. sharp, a band appeared in front of our boarding-house and forming up behind it, with the mayor and corporation bringing up the rear, we marched to the ring.

The bullfights went off well and the president handed out ears and tails regardless of what happened. We only had to kill one bull each day. It was a picnic. In the evenings Jill and I went dancing in the village square to the music of the local band. Wherever we went everything was free. It was a good life but not suitable for a bullfighter in the middle of the season. Wine, women and song are strictly off the menu during the summer but most bullfighters more than make up for it during the winter or in the odd moments they sometimes have between engagements. On the third day I began to feel the effect of my lapse from strict training and decided that on our return to La Linea I would send Jill back to England.

The people of Grazalema gave us all a terrific send-off on our way to Ronda. We had spent five very enjoyable days with them.

Ronda is a paradise. It is one of the most romantic places I know. The hotel we stayed at, the "Victoria", is perched high on the edge of a great cliff and the garden ends in a sheer drop of several hundred feet. The view from the bedrooms is breathtaking and never-to-be-forgotten. Jill was over-whelmed by the place and I realised that it was going to be a delicate job, suggesting that she should return to London.

(*Above*) Lining up to make the kill; the *muleta* is furled and the sword at eye-level. (*Photo: Mateo.*) (*Below*) The *estocada* is completed, the sword is home and soon the bull will be dead.

A *manoletina*.

Luckily it came out in the course of conversation that Peter was due back at school in a fortnight's time and I tactfully suggested that he should spend some of his holiday with his parents before the next term.

We spent three pleasant days in Ronda, during which time we met an English couple who insisted that we drove back to La Linea with them in their car. The day after arriving back, I crossed into Gibraltar and booked two seats on the first 'plane to England.

I was very sorry to see Jill and her brother leave but I had to get down to the more serious business of bullfighting. I felt empty inside after they had gone and immediately returned to the Vazquez ranch. There were several more fights booked and I resolved to stay on the ranch until the last moment and return there as soon as possible after the fights were over.

The life was clean and healthy. Some days we would spend twelve or fourteen hours in the saddle, herding the bulls. One such day we were jogging back to the ranch-house across a wide open piece of pasture when the *mayoral*, the senior cowboy, pointing to one of the seed bulls lying in the sun fast asleep, told me to ride over and wake it up in case it should get sunstroke. Without a second thought, I rode over to the large beast and gave it a prod with my lance. I have never seen anything react so quickly. In a flash it was on its feet and tearing straight for me. Luckily the horse knew what to expect and galloped off, zigzagging to avoid the onslaughts of those treacherous horns. All I could do was to hang on to the pommel of the saddle and hope to heaven that the horse would not stumble. The *vaqueros* thought it a huge joke and laughed about it for days.

Some evenings Fernando and I would sit in the rushes round a pond, situated about half a mile from the house, while he demonstrated his prowess at calling down pigeons. The birds came down each evening to drink from the pond and as soon as Fernando spotted them in the trees some distance away, he would start cooing and in no time the pigeons, thinking the coast to be clear, would fly down. Thus we added variety to our bill of fare. One evening, arriving at our hiding-place ahead of time, Fernando showed me that he had the same facility for wooing frogs. He began to croak softly and almost immediately the heads of thousands of frogs broke the surface of the pond and started to make for the bank. In a matter of minutes the ground around us was covered by the little wet creatures.

In more serious mood I would spend hours watching the bulls in their natural surroundings out on the range and I learned a great deal about them. I saw how they would spar amongst themselves. I saw which were the bullies and which were the noble fighters. Each evening at sundown, they would pair up and fight. It was very interesting to watch. They would block, parry and feint, like swordsmen. When one bull had had enough, he would simply turn his back on his opponent and amble away to look for another sparring partner. This ritual took place in a glade down by the pond. Once in a while a pair would fight in earnest and in this case the battle-ground was a dust bowl, scratched out high in the cork forests, by generations of bulls. Sensing the pending conflict, the whole herd would move up to this amphitheatre and stand as silent witnesses round the rim whilst the two adversaries fought it out in the centre.

Although the site was a good kilometre away from the ranch-house, on these occasions we would be awakened in the night by the clash of horns ringing out across the valley. Immediately we would saddle the horses, collect the steers and, riding hard for the spot, herd the bulls at a gallop to tire them. If either of the animals were injured it would have to be brought in and placed in the hospital, a narrow box the sides of which consisted of hinged flaps so arranged that the *mayoral* could get at any part of the animal which might have to be attended to.

The ranch was a romantic place, situated by the riverside and nestling in the forest amongst the foothills. At night-time I often used to sit in the deep window of my bedroom and listen to the many weird sounds of the wild. The screams of a vixen, the snorting and squealing of the wild boar, and the ceaseless croaking of the frogs. Sometimes a charcoal-burner, leading a string of soft-footed donkeys, would ride by in the moonlight, making his way into the forests of Almoraima, singing as he went a soft *flamenco* song.

During this period I experienced greater happiness than I had ever known. My life on the farm was active but very peaceful. I had no desire to go into the towns. When I fought, I would return afterwards to the ranch as soon as possible. I felt at home amongst the bulls and by watching them continuously I got to know most of them intimately. As long as they were in the herd and not too closely approached, they were harmless enough. It is when a bull becomes separated from his fellows that he is dangerous.

One evening I was returning to the ranch-house after a shooting expedition, carrying a gun in one hand and a bunch of rabbits in the other, when rounding a bend in the path I came face to face with one of the bulls. Freezing in my tracks I hurriedly debated whether or not to drop everything and shin up a tree or stand my ground and see what his next move would be. The former course was out of the question, for without turning my head I glanced sideways and saw there were no branches low enough for me to leap up to. The bull stood only ten feet away and was staring angrily at me. I could do nothing but stare back. Neither of us stirred. I longed to drop my load but knew that the slightest movement on my part would provoke the beast to charge. My arms were aching madly and I could have screamed in pain as the weight of the shotgun and rabbits tugged at the sockets of my shoulders. It was rapidly growing dark and I knew that none of the *vaqueros* would be likely to come this way. Suddenly the bull, growing bored by the situation, turned tail and trotted away, and after what seemed to be an eternity I sank to the ground exhausted.

The countryside surrounding the ranch was bandit-ridden and many times we would sleep with loaded revolvers at the side of our beds. Occasionally when riding in the hills we discovered caches of tobacco and cigarettes that had been smuggled in from Gibraltar and stacked ready for transport to the big towns and cities. There was never any sign of the bandits but one had the impression that they were continually watching. One day the two soldiers stationed on the ranch disappeared, to return a day later minus their clothes and rifles. They had wandered into the forest to do some shooting and had been ambushed by the bandits. The poor devils were worried in case they had to pay for the loss, their pay being a penny a day.

Miguel would visit me two or three times a week and one breakfast-time he arrived to show me a letter from a Spanish newsreel company saying that they had been requested by the B.B.C. Television Newsreel Service to film my next fight for them. It was a surprising request for I knew there was a great deal of antipathy in Britain towards bullfighting—most of it bred from ignorance of the subject—and the B.B.C. has always been careful not to offend public opinion.

My next fight was scheduled in Tarifa and the newsreel people were duly informed and arrangements were made for them to come down from Madrid to film it. The bullring in Tarifa is situated on the beach well below ground-level and when a *levante*, a strong east wind, is blowing it is almost impossible to manage a cape there. During the summer the *levante* blows six days out of seven, so on the morning of the fight I took an old cape with me down to the bullring to test

132

conditions. They were terrible, for the wind kept lifting the cape up into the air above my head. It would be suicidal to fight in such circumstances, and we agreed that unless the wind dropped the fight would have to be postponed.

The camera-men arrived at the hotel about an hour before the fight was due to commence and filmed the sequence of dressing, then one of them travelled in the car with the *cuadrilla* and me so that he could film us arriving at the ring. The first thing I noticed on entering was that the wind had dropped completely. It was a perfect afternoon for the fight.

My first bull was mediocre and nothing in particular was accomplished. However, my second was better and despite receiving an injury, I managed to put up a good show. It was after a *faena*, turning my back on the bull and kneeling down, throwing the *muleta* and sword aside, that I made a fatal mistake. Instead of keeping my eye on the bull, I simply rose to my feet and started to walk away from him. The next thing I knew, I was riding across the ring on his horn, before being thrown face downwards into the sand. My *banderilleros* rescued me and I managed to square the bull up and kill it before going to the *enfermeria*.

It was found that the horn had entered the rectum and torn the lower bowel but somehow the sphincter muscle had escaped serious damage. It was very painful but not too dangerous. The doctor stitched me internally under anaesthetic and kept me in bed for a couple of days before allowing me to return to La Linea to be put in the charge of the doctor there. I was soon well enough to return to the ranch but I stayed indoors most of the time. This gave me an opportunity to read some of the many books on bulls and bullfighting that Fernando Vazquez had in his library.

One of the volumes I most enjoyed was Jose Maria Cossio's encyclopaedia of bullfighting entitled "Los Toros". I was particularly interested by the section dealing with the history

133

of *tauromaquia*, telling how bullfighting had evolved from the hunting of the wild species by men on horseback in the era of the Moorish Conquest. From this developed the sport of fighting bulls from horseback, practised by the aristocracy until the early 18th century. They had their servants standing by with capes ready to act as lures in case any mishap should befall the master. The book describes how gradually the public began to enjoy the capework of the servants more than the horsemanship of their employers. It tells of the two Romeros from Ronda; of Francisco Romero, the inventor of the *muleta*, the advent of which enabled bulls to be killed with a sword from in front in much the same way as they are today; and of Francisco's grandson, Pedro, acclaimed as being the founder of professional bullfighting. I learned, too, how such great fighters as Costillares, Largartijo and Guerra had each in his turn added something to the art, and how in modern times the incomparable Juan Belmonte had revolutionised bullfighting because he was suffering from a disease that hampered his movements, forcing him to stand still and make the bull do all the work. After Belmonte, the tragic style of Manolete and the gay clowning style of Arruza had each given something to make modern bullfighting what it is today.

The one bullfighter who at that time stood out from the many was that Sevillian genius, Pepe Luis Vazquez, since whose retirement a couple of years ago there have been no great *matadores*. Bullfighting today is decadent. It has been deteriorating for years but has now reached rock-bottom. It is awaiting the coming of a new genius to lift the *fiesta* from the depths to which it has sunk. The tendency today is to encourage one-season-marvels who risk their lives clowning with the bulls and then lose either their nerve or their public, which eventually becomes bored with their trickery. The accent is on the unusual and sensational, to the detriment of classic bullfighting of the old school.

I spent a lot of time studying the herd book. It was interesting to follow the pedigree of the bulls I knew, and to read the breeder's remarks on the behaviour of their antecedents in the ring. One could judge fairly well from these records, and from the way the bulls had behaved at their testing, how they would turn out in the bullring. There were exceptions to this rule, however, as I was very soon to find out in my next fight.

My manager and I were going to promote this fight in the La Linea bullring; it was to be my last of the season and the bulls were to come from the Vazquez ranch. I spent as much time as I could studying the six animals we were buying. Amongst them was a large brown and white, with upward curving horns. I noticed that in the evenings when they paired off to spar, this particular bull was always the most aggressive and the undisputed leader of the herd. I looked up his pedigree and saw that he came from the finest stock on the ranch and had also reacted well at his testing. He had all the qualifications for being a perfect fighting-bull.

As Miguel and I were the promoters of the fight we made it a condition with the other two *matadores* contracted to appear with me, that I would not enter into the *sorteo* but would select my bulls beforehand, leaving them to draw lots to decide in what order the remaining four were to be fought. According to the law this is illegal as all bulls must be drawn for. Nevertheless, at this time a lot of *matadores* were making agreements to appear only if they could select their bulls beforehand.

Whilst the bulls were being boxed ready for transport, I remarked to the *mayoral*, who was to appear in my *cuadrilla* as a *picador*, that I had selected the large brown and white one to be in my pair.

"I shouldn't have that one if I were you, Vicente," he advised.

"But why not?" I asked. "He always acts bravely and had a good *nota* in the herd book."

"I don't like him," insisted the *mayoral*.

"But why not?" I continued. "You must have some reason."

"I can't pin it down," he answered. "My experience tells me that he will not turn out well in the ring and experience counts for a lot in this business."

I wasn't satisfied with this argument and repeated that I intended to stick by my decision. I would prove that the *mayoral* was mistaken.

In the smaller towns in Spain it is customary for the unboxing of the bulls to take place in the arena, so that the public may have a preview of the animals. To facilitate the managing of the bulls, steers are previously let into the ring and then, on the unboxing of the last bull, all are driven together into the corrals.

The preview was to be held on the Saturday night prior to the fight and a good crowd turned up to watch. When my favourite was loosed he immediately tore around the ring hooking at the people standing behind the barrier.

"There, didn't I say he was going to be good?" I said triumphantly in the direction of the *mayoral*. "His behaviour is perfect and the public obviously like him."

"I am not convinced, Vicente," he replied. "I still do not like him."

"Tomorrow will prove who is right," I said as I left him to go home to bed.

The next day just before the *sorteo* was due to begin, Fuentes, one of the other bullfighters appearing that afternoon, went to Miguel and stated that unless the bulls were sorted and drawn for according to the regulations, he refused to fight. It was too late to find a substitute for him so Miguel had to agree to his ultimatum. I drew one of the bulls I had wanted but the brown and white one fell to Fuentes. The *mayoral* was delighted.

Both my bulls were good and I was awarded the ears of each of them. The brown and white, however, turned out exactly as the *mayoral* had predicted, cowardly, treacherous and totally unfightable. Fuentes was an experienced bullfighter who had started as a child prodigy, but even he couldn't do a thing with it and barely escaped with his life. If it had been my fight I would probably not be alive today.

I had previously decided not to return to the ranch after the fight as it was now October and the end of the season. I had taken part in thirteen *corridas* and received a total of twenty-eight ears and eight tails. Now was the time to relax and enjoy a little of the gay life. I asked Miguel how much money was due to me and he gave me just over two thousand pounds, a fair sum considering the amount I had spent during the year. Apart from my own hotel expenses, I had paid all Vicente Escribano's and given him an average of ten pounds a week pocket money. I later heard that he remarked to somebody in La Linea how lucky he had been, as some people only win the National Lottery but he had done better and won an Englishman. I didn't believe this at the time, but two years later I found out just how shallow his friendship was.

There would be no more bullfighting until the next season began in the spring and I had told my parents that I would spend my Christmas in England, but before leaving Spain I decided on a pleasure trip to Madrid and invited Vicente Escribano to accompany me. We booked a couple of sleeping berths on the express and set out for a gay time in the capital.

Much to my surprise I found that the *aficion*, the fans, in Madrid had followed my season with interest and wherever Vicente and I went we were received with open arms. We stayed in Madrid for six weeks and it was just one long round of parties. Despite the fact that we were invited out most of the time, I managed to get through all my money and had to cable Miguel for my fare back to La Linea. It was incredible that so much money could have been spent in such a short time, especially as the cost of living in Madrid at that time was so low. Nevertheless at the end of six weeks I was left without a penny, having given Vicente my last few pesetas for his fare back to Valencia.

Returning to La Linea, I telephoned my father and asked him to send the money for my fare back to London. The money arrived and I booked a passage on the *Llanstefan Castle*. The ship had been on a trip round Africa and most of the passengers, tiring of the long voyage, had disembarked at Genoa and continued the last stage of their journey back to the United Kingdom overland. The few left aboard had time to kill and wanted to take full advantage of the cheap drinks available while the trip lasted. Most of the days were spent sitting in the bar yarning. Amongst my fellow passengers were gold-miners, hunters and adventurers of all categories. An outstanding storyteller was a Canadian who sported a large ginger, R.A.F.-type moustache and was known to everyone as plain "Canada".

As the ship docked at Tilbury, Canada and I were sitting in the lounge awaiting the Port Health and Immigration officials, when a newspaper reporter from one of the daily papers approached me and enquired if I was Vincent Hitchcock, the bullfighter. I replied by pointing to Canada and saying, "There's the chap you want." The reporter interviewed Canada for about twenty minutes, busily jotting down in his notebook all that the Canadian, in his best English accent, could tell him and it was not until after asking what plans he had for the coming season and my impersonator replied in his broadest Canadian that he just looked forward to "Bigger and Better Bulls", that the journalist realised he had been duped. He was furious. The poor chap had stolen a march on his rivals by managing to board the ship before it docked and now, after he had wasted so much time interviewing the wrong person, the other journalists were descending on us in a flock.

The customs formalities quickly over, I joined my parents and Pat, my sister, who were waiting for me. It was cold on the dockside and to avoid giving long interviews in such uncongenial surroundings I invited the newspapermen back to my parents' home in Southend. Whilst doing justice to a bottle or two of Scotch the reporters fired questions at me. It was my first experience of a press reception and it rather dazed me trying to answer several different questions at once whilst being photographed in my suit of lights in a hundred and one different positions. I was thankful when the last one left the house and I was able to have a quiet word with my family.

9

I DIVIDED my time between my home and the new house that Jill's parents had bought in Hurstmonceux—apart from attending a good many functions as guest of honour, a privilege which always caused me some embarrassment.

Soon after Christmas I was invited to appear on Television and also to make broadcasts to Spain in the B.B.C.'s Spanish Service. The television programme was "Picture Page" and consisted of interviews by Joan Gilbert and Leslie Mitchell. This was my first contact with television and I found it more than a little terrifying. I appeared in my bullfighting costume and that, combined with the intense brightness and heat from the lights, made it one of the most uncomfortable moments that I had experienced. It was difficult trying to converse naturally with Leslie Mitchell whilst being conscious of the cameras looming and then retreating.

A week after the television programme I received a letter from a film producer saying that he would like to see me about making a film of my story. I went to see him and was offered £50,000 to co-operate in writing the script, play my own part, and be technical adviser on the film. Foolishly I refused. I told him that having just finished my first season, I wanted to return to Spain for the coming season in order to consolidate my position there and that at the end of the following year we could discuss his proposals again. I have never forgiven myself for missing this opportunity, for when I returned to England after my next season in 1950, the film industry was going through one of its worst crises and few films were being made.

Jill was anxious for us to marry before I returned to Spain, but I realised that marriage would hamper my training and fighting, so we agreed to wait. I returned to Spain alone at the end of January.

Before leaving La Linea I had decided to make Madrid my headquarters during the coming season. Madrid is the centre of bullfighting throughout the world and I thought that it would aid me in my career if I resided there. Obviously I would have to find myself a new manager as it would be useless continuing with Miguel while he lived hundreds of miles away.

A friend of mine introduced me to Robustiano Cortes. Robustiano, who managed another bullfighter, knew very little about bullfighting but had as his adviser a well-known manager named Alejandro Graciani. I liked Robustiano, who seemed a very straightforward chap, and I signed a contract with him.

My new manager invited me to live in his house which was situated in the centre of Madrid and I gladly accepted his offer. Immediately I was installed there I began my training in earnest and went down to the Madrid ring early every morning to join the practice sessions.

It had been a pretty severe winter and the *tientas* were late in starting. The first one I was invited to was held at the ranch of Don Remi Thiebaut at Escorial, where some of the finest bulls in Spain are bred. Remi is one of the really scrupulous breeders and allows only his finest animals to go to the ring.

The night before the *tienta* I went out with an American called Lyn Goodale, to whom my manager had introduced me, and who shared my interest in bulls, good liquor and women in that order. We started drinking in the British-American Club where I was surprised to encounter antagonism from some of my compatriots, most of whom were ardent fans of bullfighting. The British living abroad usually view any fellow countryman with suspicion until they have known him for about twenty years, and these were no exceptions. They did not like the idea of me, as a new boy, being popular with the Spaniards. However, the American and I immediately became close friends. After leaving the club we wandered around the bullfighting bars in old Madrid and ended up in a little place that used to be a bullfighting school behind the Madrid bullring. We stayed there until daybreak when, with a shock, I remembered the *tienta*. Dashing home, I barely had time to bath, change into my country clothes and, clutching a cape and muleta, get down to the *Telefonica* building in time to meet Bob Gilliland of I.C.I. who was to pick me up in his car.

Before driving out to Escorial we went to the British Embassy to pick up Robin Hankey, British Chargé d'Affaires, his wife, and Juliet, his daughter. We had a drink at the Residence and then left for the ranch.

Remi's house, *El Campillo*, was built by Felipe II while he was overseeing the construction of the enormous and hideous palace, *El Escorial*. It was a severe-looking building, shaped like a matchbox on end. On the roof I noticed a pair of storks were building a nest. Remi welcomed us and took us upstairs to a spacious room off a banqueting hall. He poured us drinks and introduced Litri, a young bullfighter who had had a meteoric rise to fame the previous season. Litri and I were the only two *toreros* present. After lunch we took the cows alternately and spent a very enjoyable afternoon playing them. I was glad of the opportunity for serious training as my first fight of the season, booked for Easter Sunday in Valladolid, was not far ahead. This fight was to be my first outside Andalucia and I was anxious to see how I would be received by the less demonstrative and more serious Castillians.

On the morning of Easter Sunday I drove to Valladolid with my *cuadrilla* and arrived at the bullring just before the *sorteo* was due to begin. The bulls looked pretty good and I was eager for the fight to start. The animals turned out to be as good as I had first judged them and I was able to give a very satisfactory performance. However, my first bull gave me a couple of heavy tosses to which at the time I paid little attention but later, when undressing back at the hotel, I discovered that I had received two *puntazos*, small gores, one a hole about two inches deep in my left calf and the other right through my right leg, just under the shin bone. Both had bled very little and though I had noticed a small amount of blood on my stockings just after being hit, I had no idea of the extent of the damage and it was with amazement that I tore away pieces of blood-soaked stocking which had stuck to and plugged the wounds. My swordhandler bandaged my legs and after I had dressed we hurried to the doctor's so that I could have an anti-tetanus injection as quickly as possible. Most certainly I did not want a recurrence of the previous year's experience.

During the next few months I was kept pretty busy fighting around Castille and the north of Spain, but was anxious for my manager to sign me up for Andalucia. This came about when I was offered a contract to reappear in La Linea on the 6th June, exactly a year after my debut there and again with bulls from the Belmonte ranch.

A week before I was due to leave for La Linea I was surprised to receive a telegram from my parents telling me that they were in France and motoring down to Madrid with friends. The trip had been taken at a moment's notice and there had been no time to inform me earlier. As this was the tourist season hotel accommodation was scarce, so I arranged with Robustiano to put them up for their stay in Madrid.

As soon as they arrived I told them about the forthcoming fight and their friends, Dr. Thomas and his wife, in whose car they were travelling, said they would like to see the south of Spain and would take me down there.

We set off for Andalucia with time to spare so that we could do some sight-seeing on the way. Our first stop was Cordoba and the best part of a day was spent touring the city before moving on to Jerez. We stayed at the hotel "Los Cisnes" in Jerez and visited the sherry *bodegas* for the benefit of Dr. Thomas and his wife. There we were able to sample the contents of my own barrel before leaving for Sevilla where we inspected the Cathedral and the Alcazar and wandered around that delightful labyrinth of passages and *patios* that comprises the inimitable *Barrio de Santa Cruz*.

Arriving in La Linea late Saturday afternoon we left our luggage in the hotel and went down to the bullring with Adolfo Beaty to see the bulls unboxed. They were large and my mother, reminded of the fact that two of these beasts were to be fought by me, went back to the hotel to await us.

After my parents and Dr. Thomas and his wife had gone to bed that night, I went out alone to visit various friends whom I had not seen since the previous year. Usually before a bullfight I keep very strictly off liquor but on this occasion I accepted a glass of wine and with each renewed acquaintance, one glass led to another. Eventually I arrived back at the hotel at seven in the morning very, very tight. Pedro, who was to be my swordhandler for this fight, was waiting for me and was horrified when he saw my condition.

The fight was due to commence at 4.30 p.m. and his one concern was to get me fit in time. He ordered jugs of hot black coffee and, between my drinking these, made me take alternate hot and cold baths, making the cold ones really cold by putting large pieces of ice in the water. By midday I was very sober but feeling more dead than alive.

I deeply regretted my night's diversions, for returning to La Linea was like coming back to my home town and I was eager to triumph. With my first bull I was hopeless. I did absolutely nothing with the cape but the crowd were patient, anticipating that I would do better, as they knew that the *muleta* and sword had always been my forte and capework my weakness.

The *banderilleros* had placed the darts and it was time for me to go out for the final act. After asking the president's permission to kill, I dedicated the bull to the public—a sure way for a bullfighter to win the hearts of his audience. I walked towards the bull and, after carefully judging the distance, stood erect with my feet firmly planted together ready for the *pase de la muerte*—the pass of death. Calling the bull I shook the *muleta*, and he responded immediately, charging in my direction. Then to my horror I found my feet working independently of my brain; instead of standing still as I raised the *muleta* to let the bull pass underneath, they jumped back away from the horns. The crowd was silent. I tried again, and again it happened. Strangely enough, I couldn't attribute this to fear. Many times before, when feeling afraid, I had been able to control my nerves and limbs, but this time it was impossible. Again and again I tried, but still my feet kept jumping away as soon as the horns came close. To add to my discomfort a few of the spectators began to boo and catcall and in a little while the rest followed suit. The din was terrific. There was only one thing left to do, and lining the bull up for the kill, I attempted to go in straight over the horns; but try as I would, my feet were still completely uncontrollable and I found myself running in a half circle round the bull, stabbing at it from as far away as possible. It was after the third or fourth attempt that I managed to get the sword in and much to my relief, the bull dropped dead. By now, the whole of the bullring audience was on its feet and shouting derisively. I had to duck from the hard canvas cushions that were flung at my head as I made my way back to the barrier where Pedro was waiting with a towel to wipe the sweat from my face.

The furore gradually abated and there was dead silence which was as bad as, if not worse than, the noise. I was trying to convince myself that every bullfighter has his off days and that it was all very well for them to sit up there, safe in their seats, since not one of them would come down to the ring and do better, when suddenly a little cockney voice called out from the cheap seats on the sunny side of the ring, "Why the 'ell don't yer take up football, mate?"

I felt as if cold water had been dashed in my face. The booing of the Spaniards had passed over my head but this from a compatriot was too much. It had the right effect though and with my next bull I was able to regain some of the prestige I had lost.

Back at the hotel my parents, who had elected not to watch the fight, were waiting anxiously and I could see the relief in their faces when I walked into their room; but how humiliated and ashamed I felt when they asked me how the fight had been. To make matters worse, Robustiano came into my room whilst I was undressing and started a discourse on my bad performance.

"If it's as bad as that," I shouted at him, "I'll never fight again—never, never, never." And to lend emphasis to my words I flung my bullfighting costume out of the window into the street below. Pedro hurried downstairs to retrieve it.

"Calm down, *jefe*," he pleaded. "You must not carry on like that."

"Take it away, damn you," I bellowed at him. "Give it away. Do anything you like with it but don't let me see it again."

At that moment Dr. Thomas walked into my room and handing me a large glass of neat brandy, told me to drink it. I did so, and the shock of the fiery spirit on my sore and empty stomach brought me to my senses. I apologised to Pedro for my fit of temper and finished dressing.

The next morning we left early and after breakfasting in Malaga, journeyed on to Granada where we intended spending a few days so that Dr. Thomas and his wife might see the fabulous *Alhambra* and the beautiful gardens of *El Generaliffe* where the nightingales sing by day and night. I have never been terribly excited by historic buildings but the *Alhambra*, immersed as it is in history and romance, never fails to delight me. It is so simple and yet so complex that it summons wonderment in all who explore its intimacies. We spent two all too short days visiting and acquainting ourselves with this ancient Moorish capital and it was with regret that we had to leave for Madrid once again.

Within three days my parents were off on the road to England and I was settling quickly into training for my future fights. Every morning I used to walk to the bullring, a distance of about three and a half miles, practise there for three hours, from 9 a.m. to 12 noon, and then play *pelota* until two. *Pelota* is a ball game of Basque origin, something like squash but much faster. It is in fact rated the world's fastest game. We played it a lot because it quickens the reflexes and exercises those muscles used particularly by bullfighters. The equipment consists of a small bat, rather like a flattened baseball bat, about eighteen inches in length, and an extremely hard ball about the size of a fives ball. The speed reached by this hard ball is incredible and anyone being hit by one is in for a bad time. A simple form of *pelota* is played by women in the public *fronton* courts and the audiences bet heavily on the games. This and cock-fighting are the two most popular excuses for gambling in Spain.

On finishing the game of *pelota* I used to take a shower, change my clothes and meet my manager at one of the many *tascas*, little wine shops, that are the Madrid equivalent of the *bistros* of Paris, and over our pre-lunch glasses of wine we would discuss contracts and talk about bullfighting.

At one such meeting Robustiano told me that he had received an offer from Linares. I was pleased about this as I had long looked forward to returning to the town where my training had really started in earnest. Whilst I lived there, I had the impression that none of the locals really believed that I would ever become a *torero*, and I was delighted at this chance to disprove them. I couldn't help wondering whether they would remember me as a stocking salesman.

We travelled to Linares by train, an act of sentiment on my part for I wanted to make my return there a replica of my first visit to the place, the only difference being the omission of the long wait for the tram to take us from Baeza. My manager had arranged for a car to meet us at the station. When the car turned into the main street of Linares I received a shock. Across the street at first storey level was stretched a huge banner announcing my forthcoming appearance in the Linares ring and giving me the rather dubious title "The King of Valour." I could hardly believe my eyes but there it was sure enough in three-foot high lettering. I correctly surmised that this was the work of my friend Jose Moya, who was promoting the fight and who is well known as a sensationalist. As soon as we had settled in the hotel I called the impresario on the 'phone and demanded to know what his idea was.

"What is the matter, Vicente, don't you like it?" he asked.

"I think it stinks," I told him. "What a thing to have to live up to. Everyone will be watching me like a hawk to see if I move a centimetre away from the horns."

"Don't worry, Vicente," Jose assured me. "You have a pretty good reputation here."

"What as? A stocking seller? And what about Paco Hernandez?" I asked, referring to the other *matador*. "He's going to be hopping mad about it."

"That is the idea," said Jose triumphantly. "That is where experience as an impresario counts. To get the best out of your bullfighters all you have to do is create jealousy. It's going to be a great fight. See you at the ring. *Adios*."

148

ı slammed down the receiver. I would have to be good, otherwise I could visualise some of those stockings being wound around my neck.

Of the six bulls being fought that afternoon, two were to be despatched by a *rejoneador*. A *rejoneador* fights his bull solely on horseback. When well performed it is a magnificent spectacle, both mount and rider working in perfect unison, the result of years of meticulous training. Undoubtedly today, and some say for years, Angel Peralta is the greatest exponent of this centaurian form of fighting bulls.

Paco Hernandez did well with his first bull. It was obvious that Jose Moya's policy of piquing his *toreros* was working according to plan.

After my opening series of passes with my first animal I found the public unresponsive. It was obvious that they believed the publicity stuff and expected me to eat the bull alive. I had to work very close to the horns to raise their enthusiasm, and by doing so was awarded an ear. Paco did extremely well with his second animal and was awarded both ears. This was indeed incentive and I went out to my second determined to put up an even better show.

Finishing a series of *veronicas* with a *media-veronica*, I was walking away from the bull when a shout went up from the crowd. Turning quickly, I expected to see the beast coming straight for me but instead I saw a little boy of about ten years of age running across the sand. He had jumped into the ring from the crowd and was making straight for the bull, unfolding a *muleta* as he went. This was the first time that I had experienced the interference of an *espontaneo* or *capitalista*, as these boys are sometimes called. They are boys who, wishing to become bullfighters but never getting the opportunity of attending *tientas*, attract attention to themselves and their fighting ability by jumping into the ring during bullfights and trying to fight the bulls. The penalty for doing this is two

149

weeks in gaol and a ban from attending bullfights for a year but the gamble is worth it if some manager or impresario spots them and, bailing them out of gaol, gives them the opportunity of a contract.

This particular *espontaneo* was unlike the usual type of lad who took this chance. Mostly they are scruffy individuals who are driven in desperation to risking their lives in this way. This boy was well-dressed in white shirt and shorts with highly polished shoes and neatly combed hair. Stopping in front of the bull he spread the *muleta*, and as my *banderilleros* ran out to within a short distance of where he and the beast stood intently watching each other, he planted his feet firmly and calling the bull, executed four perfect *pases de la muerte* without moving a fraction of an inch away from the horns. The crowd went into a frenzy of applause. He continued by sending the bull away from him in a *pase de pecho*, a chest pass, and before the *banderilleros* could distract the animal's attention without endangering the little boy's life, he began a series of left-handed *naturales*. Again the crowd went into raptures over his performance. It was an amazing spectacle that this little figure created, perfectly passing a bull which stood as high as himself. On finishing the series of *naturales* he turned away from the bull and walked over to where I was standing.

"I am sorry to have poached," he apologised. Then turning on his heels he walked over to where a pair of policemen were waiting to arrest him. The cheers of the spectators now turned to boos as the policemen led him from the ring to the gaol-house.

After this wonderful show, anything that I did with the bull was lost on the public. They just were not interested.

Before we left Linares I made enquiries about the lad as I had suggested to Robustiano that we should bail him out and take him back to Madrid with us, but we were told that somebody had already looked after him. I do not know if he ever became a bullfighter or not for I never learned his name, but he certainly had the makings of a great *torero*.

Shortly after arriving back in Madrid my manager told me that I should begin preparing myself for my presentation in the capital. The thought of appearing in the great Madrid ring, first bullring of the world, awed me, and it was decided that no minor contracts should be accepted in the meantime. A friend of mine living in Madrid, an Englishman named David Erskine, learning of the approach of this severe test, invited me to go for a holiday with him and his family on the *Costa Brava* where he had rented a villa for the summer.

I spent a glorious month in the little village of Palamos swimming in the crystal-clear waters of the bay or walking through the extensive pine forests. A gipsy bullfighter, named Curro Puya (a nephew of Gitanillo de Triana), was staying at the nearby villa of Alberto Puig, a friend of ours from Barcelona, and together we used to train for three or four hours every morning. By the time the telegram arrived from my manager saying that the contract was signed I was fitter and stronger than ever and feeling ready for the formidable task of fighting before the most critical bullring public in the world. I flew back to Madrid a week before the fight was scheduled.

The bulls were to be from a herd named Batanejos. Nobody seemed to have heard of them and I wanted to know why my manager had not signed me up for a well-known breed. He assured me that these Batanejos, although relatively unknown, had a good background and should turn out well.

It was oppressively hot on Sunday, the 20th August, 1950. As I lay on my bed the sun sent brilliant shafts of light through the slits in the Venetian blinds over the windows and I watched the hands of the clock move slowly, relentlessly, on until they told me to start dressing for the ring. It was necessary to allow plenty of time as the bullring in Madrid is on the outskirts of the city and on the days of a *corrida* the traffic is too much for the inadequate roads that lead to the *Plaza de Toros*.

Our car nosed its way steadily ahead and behind us I could see the horse-drawn carriage carrying the *picadores* in the style typical of Madrid. On our arrival, the vast gates at the rear of the ring were thrown open to admit us and together with my *cuadrilla* I went straight to the chapel where we said a fervent prayer for our safety and success. As I knelt I caught a whiff of antiseptic from the *enfermeria* which adjoins the chapel, and momentarily, icy fingers of fear clutched at my stomach, but almost immediately I pushed any thoughts of possible mishap from my mind and led the way to the *patio de cuadrillas*.

It was nearly time to start and, taking our places between the *cuadrillas* of Alfonso Munoz and Vicente Escribano, we awaited the signal to begin. Then, as the gates in front of us were drawn, we looked out across the sand and I had the impression of being at the bottom of a well, the sides of which consisted of row upon row of faces stretching endlessly up to that little circle of blue high above us that was the sky. The red and yellow Spanish national flags hung lifeless on their flagpoles. These colours, which fly over every bullring in the country where a bullfight is being held, are referred to by cynical bullfighters as "old blood and pus".

The clarions sounded and the *alguacilillos* dressed in their velvet costumes and cockaded hats, a legacy from the days of Felipe II, rode out from the side of the ring to the presidential box where they asked permission for the *cuadrillas* to parade. The *alguacilillos*, apart from heading the parade across the ring, act as liaison between the president and the bullfighters and ensure that his orders (which in Madrid are telephoned down to the ringside) are carried out.

On receiving the president's acknowledgement, the horse-men rode slowly across the sand to where we were waiting and, turning in front of us, headed back across the ring again.

Stepping forward together we followed close in their wake. After exchanging our dress capes for fighting capes we slipped in behind the barrier to await the bulls.

The first one, drawn by Vicente Escribano, was good and I did a *quite* of *chicuelinas* which provoked applause from the spectators, but the second, Alfonso Munoz's, was very bad and none of us managed any fancy *quites*. When my bull came in I soon realised that it was no better than its predecessor. I attempted some *veronicas* but it kept backing up and running away. After circling the ring, trying without much success to attract its attention, I managed to get it to stand still and I motioned the *picadores* to move up.

As the first *picador* came into position I drew the bull forward towards the horse, but just as it charged a gust of wind caught the cape and wrapped it around my legs. The bull, seeing this movement, hooked in following the cape and I was sent spinning through the air to crash under the horse. As the bull came at my fallen body, the *picador* shot out his lance to deflect the charge and the bull, turning, hit the horse and together they crashed on top of me. My *banderilleros* rushed in to lead the bull away from the mêlée whilst the bullring attendants pulled the horse off me, but as the animal regained its feet a hoof hit me in the head. By the time I had been dragged out from under its legs I was feeling very dazed and not at all sure of my whereabouts. My swordhandler bathed my head whilst the *banderilleros* placed the darts, and when the signal came for the last act to begin, I had recovered to some extent. After trying desperately to get the bull to charge the *muleta*, I decided that the only thing to do was to kill it and hope that my next one would be better. The animal had taken up a defensive position hard against the barrier and it was with difficulty that I got the sword home.

The next three beasts were no better than the preceding two and my second animal, the last of the afternoon, gave me no opportunity of accomplishing anything outstanding. I was very upset not to have had the success that I had hoped for in Madrid. I found that it was often when I hoped most for success that it seemed furthest away.

The following morning Robustiano told me that the bull-ring management had offered me another fight on the next Sunday but he had demurred, saying that it would be better for me to have a few more fights in the provinces to restore my confidence. I did not agree with this idea but decided that I would leave it to him.

Later that week I was offered a contract to appear in Valencia, but before accepting it I suggested to my manager that he should travel down there and take a look at the bulls. He too agreed that the animals should be inspected; however, being unable to leave Madrid, he asked Alejandro Graciani to go in his stead. The following day I received a telephone call from him saying that he had seen them and that they were fine. On the strength of this information I collected my *cuadrilla* and together we took the train to Valencia.

It was well into the evening when we arrived at the station and Alejandro met us from the train. I told him that I would like to go straight to the bullring, which is in the centre of the town and practically next door to the station, but he said it was too late and that the caretaker had already left the ring. I was not in the least suspicious and willingly agreed to leave it until the morning.

The morning was half gone when I awoke the next day and after I had finished the egg and milk which constituted my sole meal before a *corrida*, I went to look for Alejandro. The hall porter at the hotel told me that he thought my *cuadrilla* had gone over to the bullring for the *sorteo*. Hurrying in the direction of the *Plaza de Toros*, I arrived at the gate where the bullfighters enter, to see Alejandro and the *cuadrilla* coming out.

"Have they finished the *sorteo*?" I enquired.

"Yes," answered Alejandro, "I thought you would be better sleeping so I did not bother to call you."

"And what of the insects in there?" I asked my *banderillero de confianza*, indicating the corrals. "Are they any better than the Madrid lot?"

"They are like elephants, *jefe*," interrupted Antonio the *picador*.

"Shut up," said Alejandro savagely. "Every bull looks like an elephant to you these days. Are you afraid of taking a little fall on that thick skull of yours?"

"But they are like the old-time bull," insisted Antonio. "Like the cathedrals of the pre-*peto* days," he said, referring to the days before the horses wore protective padding in the ring—the days when concussion and broken bones were everyday affairs to the men who plied Antonio's trade.

"Are they really big?" I asked Alejandro with some anxiety.

"Like *autobuses* and with horns like this," interposed Antonio before Alejandro could reply. He held his arms sideways at full length with his fingers pointing upwards to indicate the size of the horns.

"I told you to shut up, you big windbag," shouted Alejandro angrily.

I could see that a row was imminent and hurriedly suggested that we should go to the café for a lemonade.

"Come on then," said the *picador*, "but it's not going to be lemonade for me. I need a brandy."

In the café Alejandro tried to reassure me.

"The bulls are big, Vicente," he admitted, "but it is all fat. You'll see, they will be like lambs after they have run around a little."

"Anyway they are the same size for the three of us," I said, referring to the other two bullfighters appearing with me.

"Oh, by the way, the boys supposed to be fighting with

you this afternoon have gone sick and two local lads will be taking their places," Alejandro informed me.

I did not like this news. It is common practice for *toreros*, when they wish to break their contract, to get a certificate from a not-too-particular doctor, and in this case I guessed that the respective managers had seen the bulls and reckoned that they were not for their lads. We finished our drinks and I returned to the hotel to rest.

When it was time for me to start dressing, the usual stream of wellwishers began to drop in to wish me luck for the afternoon, but instead of the usual banter about the wonderful little bulls they all asked the same question: "Had I seen the animals?" I began to get worried, and by the time I arrived at the ring I was in a state of near panic.

All bullfighters feel scared before the fight commences. Some are actually physically sick with fear, but when the first step is made across the sand, their fears are forgotten. I had been through this many times before and often at that moment I had sworn never to fight again, but once I found myself out there with the bull, it was the finest thing in the world and after the fight was over I could hardly wait for the next to begin. Belmonte expressed it well when he said that if a bull-fighter had to sign his contracts on the morning of the *corrida*, there just wouldn't be any more bullfighters.

It will be all right once the parade starts, I told myself as I waited, anxious for the trumpet to give the signal for the proceedings to begin. The trumpet sounded and we moved forward across the ring in the parade, but instead of diminishing, my fear increased. I think if it had been at all possible I would have turned and run, but it was too late. I would have to see it through.

As senior *matador* I had to take the first and fourth bulls and it was with anxiety that I watched the gate swing open to admit the first beast. It trotted in and stood in the centre of the ring. It was big, far bigger than any I had yet faced, but it was not the enormous animal I had been expecting. I did some mediocre *veronicas* and the *picadores* moved into position. The first *picador* was the reserve, supplied by the bullring management, and he moved in confidently, anxious to make the most of his opportunity. He never touched the bull. Before he could sink the steel of the *pic* into its shoulders he was flat on the ground with the horse on top of him.

Moving in quickly, I attracted the bull away from the fallen rider and mount. I made no fancy passes but just drew the beast away to a distance of about five yards and kept its attention until the *picador* was helped back into the saddle. Then I led it back in front of the horse and the whole catastrophe was repeated.

Motioning to Antonio to move in, I caped the bull over towards him. Antonio was more experienced, keeping close to the fence when the bull charged, and sank the steel deep into its shoulders before he too was brought down. As one of the other *toreros* made his *quite*, leading the bull away from the horse, the trumpet sounded for the *picadores* to clear out of the ring.

It was impossible. I was nonplussed. A big bull like that with only one *pic*. Looking across the sand I saw the beast standing with head held high and tail swishing violently. It was as fresh as when it had entered the ring.

The *banderilleros* placed the darts swiftly and it was time for me to go out to kill. I walked over and asked the president's permission to start the third act. Meanwhile my *cuadrilla* were trying to make the bull stand in one position, but the animal was obviously master of the situation. It was hooking at their capes and sending them high into the air. Cautiously, I moved towards those murderous horns.

As the bull came towards me, I swept the *muleta* out in a *pase por bajo*, describing a wide arc to take the horns well clear

157

of my body and enable me to see how the animal would follow the lure. Instead of following the *muleta*, it stopped dead half-way through the charge and hooking at the cloth, sent it spinning out of my hands. I dashed for the barrier with unnecessary haste, for the bull did not attempt to follow me but instead stood where I had left him and continued to destroy the *muleta*. My swordhandler passed me another over the barrier and I turned once again to face my formidable adversary. I determined not to attempt a *faena* but simply to make a kill. After several short chopping passes and twice more being disarmed, I had the bull standing still and rapidly raised my sword and went in to kill, but the animal anticipated this move and hooked out before I could make the thrust. I tried again and again. I was getting desperate and hardly noticed the trumpet sound the warning that I was taking too long; my ten minutes were up and I had only another five in which to dispose of the beast. I managed to drive the sword home with my next attempt and, as I did so, a sharp pain cut through my right hand. Looking down I saw that the wrist joint of my thumb was out. Leaving my *banderilleros* to keep an eye on the bull, I walked to the barrier to show my sword-handler, who promptly grasped my thumb and jerked it across the top of the fence. I yelled as the bone slid back into place but was grateful for this effective if crude remedy. Turning to look at the bull, I saw it was where I had left it and showing no signs of dropping. The red hilt of the sword protruded from the black mass of its shoulders. Indicating to my swordhandler to pass me the *descabello* sword, I walked back to the bull as the second warning sounded, and knew that I had a bare two minutes in which to finish it.

Holding the *muleta* low over my right knee which was bent forward, I made the bull drop its head, exposing the vulnerable spot in the back of its neck, but to my dismay I discovered that I couldn't grip the sword with my right hand. Desperately

158

I attempted to raise the weapon, but it was impossible. The third and final warning sounded and I turned away from the bull knowing that I would not be allowed to touch it again. The gates to the pens were thrown open for the steers to come in and herd the bull to the corrals. I was about to experience the ignominy of having a bull removed alive from the ring.

Deep down inside me I felt sick, not with fear but with disgust at myself. Always I had prided myself on my ability to kill cleanly and well, and now this had happened. I raised my head from the barrier and looked across at the bull. The steers were entering the ring now and the bull still stood, swaying on its feet, and then suddenly it crashed to the sand, dead. It was with relief that I watched the steers returned to the corrals and the mule team enter to drag the carcase from the ring.

Before the second bull was loosed, I walked to the *enfermeria* to have my hand attended to. The doctor ran his expert fingers over the member, and, concluding that no bones were fractured, he bandaged it and told me I could return to the ring. I was half-hoping that he would say there was sufficient damage to prevent my continuing the fight, but he obviously didn't consider the injury to be very serious.

Soon after I had resumed my position behind the barrier the boy who was to kill the second bull was caught and gored in the eye. As he was carried to the *enfermeria* in the arms of his *banderilleros*, I took my sword and *muleta* and stepped into the arena. It was my obligation as senior *matador* to kill his bull for him. I despatched it with one thrust.

After the remaining *matador* had killed the third bull there was the usual break whilst the watercart entered the ring to damp down the sand. I waited until it had finished its circuit and then took my place to await my second bull.

The door of the bull-pens yawned open and for a moment nothing was to be seen. Then suddenly the largest pair of horns that I have ever seen on a bull appeared in the portal. I later found out that they measured nearly a yard and a half from point to point. Behind the horns came the bulk of the bull's body. It was a colossus and I swear that as he left the darkness of the pens he paused, and looked me straight in the eye.

My entrails seemed to turn to water as I stepped out to await the onslaught of this elephantine monster. Antonio had been right: surely no *autobus* could be larger than this thing now confronting me.

My *banderilleros* made small show of running the animal and it was clear that they too were in a panic. I made a couple of passes, scuffling my feet backwards in the sand as I did so. The *picadores* on their scraggy mounts crept up reluctantly. The bull charged the horses five times before feeling the first bite of the *pic* in its shoulders. We did our *quites* as hurriedly as possible and several times narrowly averted disaster befalling the defenceless horsemen. Antonio contrived to sink the *pic* and bore down on it as if to settle a personal score with the bull. He had been thrown four or five times and was feeling in a vicious mood. The bull received four *pics* before the *picadores* were signalled from the ring; then, after the darts were placed, I went out to kill, convinced that this bull would either leave the ring alive or catch me in the process of killing it.

Without attempting a *faena* I squared the bull up and went in over the horns, expecting to feel one of them tear into my body. Then the bull was gone and I was left with only the *muleta* in my hand. The great beast wavered, turned to face me and tumbled over, its four feet in the air. Weak with relief, I walked back to the barrier as a scattered round of applause broke from the audience who were by this time bored by the afternoon's debacle.

Apart from making a couple of *quites* with the next two bulls, my job was over, and I felt that a great load had been

(*Right*) A narrow escape, where the bull misjudged his distance and finished by somersaulting over me. (*Below*) On the steps of Juan Belmonte's ranch-house with the great maestro himself.

(*Above*) Leaving Algeciras bullring with ears and tail the day I reappeared after my first goring. (*Below*) Talking to an *aficionado* and well-known bullfighters' tailor before my presentation in Madrid.

lifted from me as I slid behind the barrier to speak to Alejandro. I had plenty to say to him. Searching the faces of the people standing in the *callejon* I could see no sign of him, so I asked my swordhandler if he knew his whereabouts and learned that he had left the ring after the first bull. This to my mind was a sure admission of guilt.

It was up to the next *matador* to kill both the remaining bulls; the fifth originally intended for our injured companion and the sixth, which was his own. It was while passing the fifth bull with the *muleta* that the other boy was caught and instantly carried to the *enfermeria* bleeding profusely from a deep gore in the thigh.

My morale was certainly not boosted by this turn of events and with trepidation I realised that as sole remaining *matador* it was my duty to kill the last two bulls. I made short work of despatching them and it was with amazement at my own good fortune that I walked from the ring, unscathed, apart from my injured thumb.

The most bloody and nerve-wracking afternoon I have known was now over.

10

CHRISTMAS in Madrid is wonderfully gay. Not the feasting and drinking *en famille* that we know here in England, but a *fiesta* which is carried into the streets. One cannot walk in the centre of the town on *Noche Buena*, the night of Christmas Eve, without being invited to drink from dozens of proffered bottles. The *Puerta del Sol*, Madrid's Piccadilly Circus, becomes a seething mass of enjoyment-bent humanity.

Allowing myself to be swept by the tide of the festivities helped obliterate the memories of the fiasco in Valencia which had terminated my 1950 season. As a result of that fight my manager had refused the offer of a contract guaranteeing a minimum of six *corridas* in *Mexico*. Three in Mexico City and three in the frontier town of Tijuana. I was very disappointed at missing this opportunity but the wisdom of my manager's decision was all too apparent. Once the slide downhill has begun it is not easy to stop. It would be better for me to spend the winter in Spain, fighting at the *tientas*, than to risk making a poor debut on the other side of the Atlantic.

The festivities of Christmas came to an end on the night of January 6th, *Dia de los Reyes*, the Day of the Kings, which is the Spaniards' equivalent of our December 25th, when the family parties are held and the children receive their gifts.

With the holidays gone, my thoughts turned to the coming *tientas*. The weather had remained mild and they were sure to begin early. I trained hard every day and looked forward to getting to grips with the cattle once again. Then came the snow.

It was my first experience of snow in Spain and I found that, as with the heat in the summer, the antipodal season lacked nothing in intensity. The first snowflakes started to fall at four-thirty in the afternoon; by seven o'clock a veritable blizzard raged. It continued most of the night, and when it stopped, several feet of snow lay on the ground. Over two thousand trees had been brought down in the capital, either by the force of the wind or the weight of the snow.

By morning the air had cleared, the wind had dropped, and once again the skies were blue and crystal clear. I decided to go for a walk in the *Retiro*, Madrid's large park. How different it was from the summer when I had rowed on its rectangular artificial lake and seen the soldiers flirting with the nursemaids. Gone were the watersellers and photographers; the few brave peanut vendors who remained huddled behind their stalls in an effort to keep warm.

The snow and ice had hung a million sparkling jewels on the black filigree of the bare trees. Now and then a branch would give way under the weight of its burden and, with a resounding crack, send a fluffy cascade earthwards.

"Aren't you going to England this year?" Robustiano enquired one day.

"I hadn't thought about it but if this sort of weather is going to continue for long I'll most certainly go over and see my parents for a few weeks," I replied.

Shortly after this I booked a seat on a 'plane and left for England. My father had been unwell with heart trouble and I knew that it would cheer him up if I spent some time with him. Also I was anxious to clear up the position between Jill and myself. Her letters were becoming cool and I had not written to her at all for some weeks. I still didn't fancy the idea of marrying and thought that it would be of mutual benefit if we discussed and clarified our relationship.

After spending a fortnight with my parents, I went down

163

to Hurstmonceux to see Jill. We discussed our future and decided to break the engagement. I returned to Spain free from worry and determined to dedicate myself entirely to my profession, and to forget about serious romance for a year or two.

I arrived in Madrid to find the weather had improved and Spring was in the air. Spring in Madrid is even more invigorating than its proverbial counterpart in Paris and its advent was like a tonic to me, making me eager to get back into the old routine.

During my absence Robustiano had decided to cease his managerial commitments and devote all his attention to other business activities. Automatically I passed into the care of Alejandro Graciani and, despite the Valencia affair, I knew I was in good hands. There are few who know more about bulls than he.

To make a break from training in the bullring every day, I would sometimes go to the *Casa del Campo*, a natural park on the outskirts of Madrid where, from a small hill, there is a perfect panoramic view of the capital. Here, too, the ground bears stark testimony to the ravages of that fateful siege during the Spanish Civil War.

On other mornings I would go for long runs in the pine woods of *La Dehesa de la Villa*. Everywhere the buds were bursting and the crocuses pushing up their coloured heads. The woods were full of the songs of birds and I would watch flocks of goldfinches arriving, ready to pair up and mate. The tropical-coloured bee-eaters flashing through the trees and the crested hoopoes' bounding flight created diversions which helped to break the tedium of out-of-season training.

Already the *tientas* were being held and I paid several visits to *El Campillo*, the ranch of my friend Remi Thiebaut. I trained with Antonio Ordoñez, third son of the famous *Niño de la Palma*. Antonio is a good *matador* and pure in style. It is strange that in so many bullfighting families the third son becomes the best *torero*. It is the same with the Dominguins and the Bienvenidas. Luis Miguel Dominguin stands out way ahead of his brothers, as does Antonio Bienvenida in relation to his.

About this time, I spent a number of evenings at the British-American Club, playing snooker. One such evening I was playing in a foursome with my American friend, Lyn Goodale, as partner, when a tall willowy blonde walked through the snooker room and into the bar, which on the night of the weekly dance was open to women members. As she passed I remarked to Lyn that we would have to get ourselves introduced, but we continued playing and it was just as I had sunk the black that Frank Porter, a chap whom I knew slightly, came out of the bar and said that he would like to introduce me to someone who wanted to meet me. Taking me to the blonde he said:

"Here you are, Jacquie, you said you wanted to meet a bullfighter. This is Vicente." He then introduced me to Jacqueline Makepeace.

I said the customary "How do you do?"

"You speak English!" said Jacqueline, astonished.

"But why not? I am English," I replied.

"I thought you said he was a bullfighter," she said, turning to Frank Porter.

"Oh he's a bullfighter all right but he happens to be English," Frank replied.

"I never knew Englishmen went in for that sort of stuff," Jacqueline said to me. "I think it's beastly. How you can go out there and stab a poor bewildered little bull to death, I really don't know. I would like to do the same to you."

This was my cue. The rest of the evening was spent in convincing her that the bulls were neither poor, little nor bewildered. By the time the club closed she was very interested and I promised to take her to see a bullfight on the following Sunday.

We were fortunate in that the *corrida* was a good one and Jacqueline was able to appreciate the points I had made. She enjoyed it and said that she would like to go again. We went on three consecutive Sundays before she had to return to Paris.

In return for my having taken her to the bullfights, she invited me to the film studios where she was "dubbing" a Spanish film with English dialogue. Small sections of it were run through time and again until the English words fitted exactly the Spanish mouthings and actions. This was a new and interesting experience for me, especially when I was given a small part to play.

About this time there seemed to be an influx of international film people into Madrid and through meeting a number of them my interest in films was roused and again it was brought home to me that I had missed a wonderful opportunity in refusing the offer to play my own part in a film about my start as a bull-fighter. Amongst the first of the English contingent with whom I became particularly friendly was producer Eric L'Epine Smith, a culinary enthusiast who spent what spare time his business allowed him, searching for and sampling new dishes and recipes to add to his already extensive repertoire.

When the time came for Jacqueline to return to Paris, I accompanied her to the airport and before leaving she said that she would be coming back to Madrid to stay. My first fight of the season was signed up for a fortnight's time and I was sorry that she could not stay on to watch it as I didn't take her promise to return very seriously.

The fight turned out to be neither a failure nor the success with which I had hoped to begin the new season. I was tossed by the first bull after making a favourable start, and falling heavily, received multiple fractures of my right collar bone. Instead of the usual arm support used in the case of such fractures, my two shoulders were firmly held back by a plaster bandage which was wound in a figure of eight over the shoulders, under the armpits and across the back. It was very uncomfortable and cramping but I was assured by the surgeons that it was by far the most effective means.

This was my most frustrating injury, not the usual open wound and hospitalisation, but mobile discomfort which allowed me to make tantalising visits to watch bullfights.

Fortunately for me, Jacqueline did return to Madrid. I received a telephone call from her one afternoon saying that she had arrived at the airport. I quickly took a car and went out to meet her. She was most concerned over my injury and nursed me tenderly until the plaster was removed. Thirty days was the time given by the doctor to allow a perfect set but it was nearer forty days before this was accomplished. By that time we had entered June and the beginning of the heat. The plaster had bitten deep into my flesh under each arm and the sweat kept running into these wounds and irritating them terribly. I don't know what I would have done without Jacqueline who dressed them for me frequently.

As time passed, our friendship deepened. My arm was recovering its strength and Jacqueline would accompany me to the bullring to watch me practise. I taught her one or two passes and found that she had a natural aptitude for handling a cape and *muleta*. Little by little her ability increased with practice as did her knowledge of bullfighting through watching *corridas* every Sunday in the Madrid ring.

This talent of Jacqueline's led me to suggest that I should train her, and perhaps get a contract for her to fight in public in either Portugal, France or Morocco, where women are allowed to fight on foot. This is illegal in Spain where they are only allowed to fight as *rejoneadoras*, equestrian bullfighters. As soon as she seemed fairly proficient I arranged for her to go with me to a *tienta* so that I would be able to see how she

167

would react in front of the horns. Jacqueline was very excited at the thought of fighting a real animal but as the day of the *tienta* approached I began to grow apprehensive and at the last minute cancelled the whole project. I realised I was much too fond of her to allow such a risk of injury.

A contract was signed for me to fight in Palma de Mallorca and I looked forward eagerly to the prospect of getting back into the ring. I had never visited Palma but having heard much about its beauty I was excited at the thought of going there. It was arranged that the *toreros* should travel by ship from Valencia and take the bulls with us. I went down to Valencia station with Pepe Monllor, the impresario, to help unload the bulls and see them safely stowed on the deck of the ship. They were travelling as bulls always travel, in individual boxes. We arrived at the dockside and found that there were no dockers available but we managed to find a crane driver. As I had had some experience whilst in the Merchant Navy of loading deck cargoes, I went on board and signalled instructions to the driver of the crane. Standing on the gunwale of the ship I waved the boxes down into position. We had five of them in place and the sixth was suspended over the deck when it suddenly swung round towards me. Without thinking, I stepped back to avoid it and fell straight into the sea. The dockers arrived on the quayside just in time to see me emerge from the water, covered from head to foot in flotsam.

The *Plaza de Toros* of Palma, a stone building rather like a Roman amphitheatre in appearance, was packed on the day of the fight. I was lucky in my first bull and was awarded the ear and made two circuits of the ring to receive the applause. After the third bull, it had been arranged that I would present the cup to the local football team who had won their divisional championship. It is surprising the compatibility that exists between footballers and bullfighters. Most footballers are keen fans of the *corrida* and most bullfighters are ardent followers of football and passionately support their home teams. The two seasons very slightly overlap, as do those of football and cricket in this country.

My second bull was large and slate-grey in colour. After the first few passes, I noticed that he was partially blind in the right eye and consequently hooked in on that side so that he could follow his target with his good eye. I did a *faena* based on left-handed passes and then lined the bull up to kill.

There was no way in which I could avoid the right horn in killing—whether left-handed or right-handed, *matadores* always make the swordthrust over the right horn. As I leaned forward, pushing the sword blade out of sight in the great hump of tossing muscle, the bull raised its head and hooked in towards me, catching me in the right armpit. I felt a sharp pain in my shoulder, the one that had recently healed, and immediately I thought that the bone had been broken again. Without waiting to see if the bull was dead, I ran in great pain to the *enfermeria*, supporting my right arm in my left hand as I did so. The doctor soon discovered the cause of the pain. The horn had knocked the top of my upper arm bone out of the socket. With a little pulling and pressure applied in the right places he clicked the offending bone back into position. It remained tender for a long time and the doctor advised me to rest it well before attempting to fight again. This was a serious setback as the season was, by this time, well under way and I had already lost a number of contracts through the first accident.

On my return to Madrid I consulted my own doctor and he examined me thoroughly, confirming what I had been told in Palma, that I needed to rest. My doctor was a personal friend and very keen on bullfighting. He was a professor at the Madrid General Hospital and used to allow me into the operating theatre to watch him operate, and into the dissecting room to watch the autopsies. I had always been keen on medicine and it had been my boyhood dream to become a surgeon, but when given the opportunity of entering Liverpool University to start my studies, I had impulsively decided to go to sea instead. My friend would go to great lengths to describe the damage done by various horn wounds and would demonstrate on the bodies in the dissecting room the different nerves and arteries that would or could be affected. This fascinated me and allowed me to form a more objective view of gorings.

My enforced inactivity gave me a wonderful opportunity of showing Jacqueline Madrid. We spent hours looking at the fabulous Prado collection of paintings. We visited the house of El Greco in Toledo and saw the famous murals and tapestries of the barrack-like palace of El Escorial. We visited the lush and verdant Aranjuez and ate unbelievably tender asparagus in the open-air restaurants on the banks of the Tagus. At night we would dine in the many and varied restaurants of Madrid. Tiring of eating formal meals, we would sometimes buy bread, onions, tomatoes and some sausage or shellfish and take them to the bar of a friend of ours, an *ex-matador* named Antonio Sanchez who had been gored out of bullfighting years ago. There we would eat our food and drink litres of his good white wine drawn straight from the barrel. When Antonio had been forced to retire from the profession, his artistic talents had looked for another means of expression and he had taken up painting. As proof of his self-developed faculty, the bar was hung with his paintings—mainly portraits of subjects dear to Antonio's heart, the typical people of Madrid; the bootblacks, the match vendors and the old men in their knee-length winter capes. The pictures were excellent but though he had received many offers for them he refused to sell, saying that he received more pleasure from having them around him than he would from the money.

Antonio himself is the personification of the Spanish *Caballero*. His wavy white hair tidily combed, he is always immaculately dressed, extremely gentle and courteous, and endears himself to all who meet him. We would listen enraptured to his tales of the bullring of old and his descriptions of customs and scenes of bygone days. Some of our most enjoyable moments were spent in his company and as we left his tavern we would often see him at the door, passing round a large wine-skin full of wine to the poor of the district.

The more Jacqueline saw of Spain, the more she fell in love with it. I was pleased to think that she shared my sentiments on the subject and was so enthusiastic about the country and its customs. She was eager to see more of it and I promised that I would take her with me to my next fight which was to be in the area known as *La Mancha*.

Before leaving for Villarrobledo where the fight was due to take place, I was warned that the public would prove to be tough. The small town was set in the windmill-hunting ground of Don Quixote and evidently the people there were not averse to tilting against bullfighters they considered to be fighting too far away from the horns.

Although I told Jacqueline what to expect, she was adamant in her decision to accompany me. She argued that it would be a wonderful opportunity for her to see another part of Spain and another facet of the Spanish character. We travelled down on the night train, arriving at our destination in the early hours of the morning. The only means of transport from the station was a creaking carriage, drawn by a tired horse. Clip-clopping our way to the hotel we took a quarter of an hour to cover a journey which we could easily have made on foot in ten minutes. With the arrival of so many visitors who had come into town for the *corridas*, the hotel was overcrowded and we were informed that no room had been booked for Jacqueline, so a cot was improvised for my swordhandler in my room and she had the one reserved for him.

After an early breakfast, we went to the bullring to see the bulls. It was with a shock that we looked down into the corral, for the animals enclosed there were huge and about four or five years of age. We were not using *picadores* in this fight and it is against the regulations covering bullfighting to fight bulls of such size and age without *picadores*.

Pepe Monllor, who was representing me for this *corrida*, was furious at what he saw and sent for the impresario of the bullring, demanding to know what the idea was in getting bulls like these for such a *corrida*. The impresario insisted that the bulls were all right, but Pepe disputed this and said that unless we were paid more money the contract was off.

"But you will have to fight now," the impresario blustered. "You have signed the contract and there is nothing to be done about it."

"Where is the veterinary surgeon's certificate?" demanded Pepe.

All bulls have to be inspected and certified by a veterinary surgeon before they can be fought in public and the *matadores* are within their rights in demanding to see the certificate.

"The vet. saw the bulls earlier this morning and said they were all right," mumbled the impresario. "He is going to send the certificate down later."

Pepe was adamant. "No certificate; no fight," he told the impresario, who by this time was really worried. It was the annual fair in Villarrobledo and he knew that if the fight did not take place the populace would be in an ugly mood and out for his blood.

"If you don't fight I'll have you thrown in gaol," he threatened me.

There was a policeman standing nearby and turning to him I said: "Come on, you must arrest me now." Taking the policeman by the arm, I led him towards the gate leading from the bullring. He protested.

"You heard what has been said," I told him. "I refused to fight and now you must arrest me."

"But I can't," he pleaded. "There is no charge." He looked nervously towards where the impresario and Pepe were standing.

"That's right," said Pepe. "You have heard what the señor here has said. You must arrest Vicente, and me too."

The impresario, seeing that we were serious, immediately changed his attitude.

"Vicente," he pleaded, "you must fight. If not I'll be ruined."

"And what about me?" I answered. "I'll be ruined too if one of those grey-bearded *bichos* in there gets its horns into me, and it won't be financial ruin for me but physical ruin for life."

"I'll pay you more money if you promise to appear this afternoon," he promised.

"It isn't a question of money," I answered. "More than that it is the principle of the thing. You must have had murderous intentions when you bought this lot," I added, hooking my thumb at the corrals.

It wasn't my place to discuss the question of money with him and I turned away to where Jacqueline was standing following the proceedings with wide-eyed amazement. I left it in Pepe's capable hands to haggle over the amount I should receive, and, taking Jacqueline by the arm, I led her away from the bullring.

As we walked back to the hotel she said: "I thought there was going to be a fight. What was it all about? I missed a lot of it as you were all talking so fast and excitedly."

I explained what had taken place at the ring. "Wait until this afternoon," I said. "There may be fireworks during the *corrida*. Juanito Posado, Montero and Pedres, fought here yesterday and the public started to wrench up stones from the seats and pelt the *toreros*. About thirty people were arrested and locked up as a result."

"Do you think that might happen this afternoon then?" she asked, alarmed.

"I sincerely hope not," I smiled. "The *comisario* has given strict instructions that anybody hurling brickbats at the bullfighters will be very severely dealt with. Having vented their spleens yesterday I think they will probably remain pacific today."

We were passing a corner thronged with men dressed in the short smocks that appeared to be the inevitable dress of the locals. They all wore black berets flat on their heads and pulled well down over their eyes and all carried canes. As we passed, some of them called out to me, shaking their sticks and saying unsmilingly, "You had better fight close this afternoon." I knew what they meant.

"It looks as if I spoke too soon," I said to Jacqueline. "If I don't put up a performance today I'll probably have to ask for police protection leaving the ring."

"Surely you are not serious?" she enquired incredulously. "They wouldn't really touch you, would they?"

"I wouldn't like to bet on it. Only last season in a town north of Madrid, the public grabbed a *torero* after the fight and carried him through the streets shoulder high in mock triumph and then dumped him in the river, still in his costume."

With these unquiet thoughts I entered the hotel and went up to my room to rest.

A seat had been reserved for Jacqueline in the front row beside Pepe and I had promised to hand her up my dress cape and dedicate a bull to her. During the parade across the ring my eyes searched the ringside seats but I could not see her. After bowing to the president, I slipped off my cape and continued to look, but to no avail. Then I spotted a couple of very beautiful Spanish girls sitting together so I passed my cape to them. Jacqueline was rightly furious; she had been sitting only six or seven seats away. It is said that a bullfighter cannot even recognise his own mother just before he goes to the ring, and I came to the conclusion that there is some truth in the observation.

Before the fight started, two or three of the bullring attendants circled the ring bearing placards stating that if there was a repetition of the previous day's happenings, the fight would immediately be suspended and the offenders clapped in gaol. There were no untoward incidents.

The bulls turned out to be brave and attacked repeatedly with little provocation. My first animal was the larger of my two, but despite his size he proved to be very manageable. I did three distinct *quites* before the trumpets sounded for the darts to be placed.

After dedicating the bull to Jacqueline, I started my first *faena* with two *pases por bajo*, passes in which the *muleta* is swept out in a low arc, at the end of which it is snatched from before the horns and then immediately pushed forward into the bull's withers, making it double back sharply on to itself. The effect of this pass is to tire the bull (in this case, to take the place of the absent *picadores*); it also keeps the *muleta* in front of the bull's eyes all the time and gives it an obvious target.

The bull reacted to this treatment and lost a lot of its previous freshness. I did a series of right-handed passes bringing the bull round and round me in a tight clockwise circle, and then at the end of the eighth pass I changed the *muleta* over to my left hand behind my back and swept the horns past my chest and away from me in a *pase de pecho*. The stands exploded in a roar of applause and I looked up to where Jacqueline was sitting. She smiled and nodded her approval.

After two more series of right-handed passes, I created a *faena* of left-handed passes, the horns scraping my stomach as the bull charged time and again. After ten left-handed *naturales*, I finished off with a left-handed *molinete*, spinning between the horns with the cloth of the *muleta* wrapped round my waist by the body of the animal as it roared past. Looking up at the public I saw that people were standing up in their seats waving handkerchiefs. They were asking the president to give me the ears before I had even killed.

Following a *faena* of *manoletinas* the audience was frantic and I made another four passes with my eyes glued to the stands without looking at the bull at all. The applause was terrific and I knew that the time had come for me to kill. Leading the bull over to in front of where Jacqueline was sitting, I carefully squared it up; then, throwing away the *muleta*, I took a pocket handkerchief from the inside of my waistcoat and, using this tiny lure, went in over the horns to bury my sword in the bull's shoulders. The beast passed so close that my feet were lifted off the ground but I managed to maintain my balance. It coughed twice and collapsed to the sand with a thud that shook the stands.

My *banderilleros* handed me the ears and the tail and turning from where I was standing by the barrier, I held the trophies aloft for the president's approval. He nodded and I bowed my thanks before starting on a circuit of the ring. The public showered in everything, hats, coats, cigars, wine-skins, the lot. I was forced to circle the ring three times before finally retiring behind the barrier. I handed the two hairy triangles and the tail up to Jacqueline as mementos of the occasion.

The success I had achieved with my first bull made me feel on top of the world. This had been my best fight since before my presentation in Madrid and I looked forward anxiously to my second animal, determined to do the same, if not better.

Immediately my *banderillero de confianza* began to run the second bull I knew that my hopes would not be fulfilled, for every time the bull reached the cape it leapt with its forelegs off the ground and hooked in viciously towards the *banderillero's* body. He was lucky to escape having its horn smashed into his face.

Determined to do the best I could, I started a series of *veronicas*. At the first one, the horn whistled past my head and the bull turned in quickly to come at me again. I swept my hands out as far away as possible from my body, at the same time trying to keep them low; then everything exploded and I was lying on my back in the sand with the wet muzzle of the bull pushing into my face. The *banderilleros* drew the beast away from me before the horn could find my body again. I clambered to my feet and found that apart from a small cut and a few bruises I was unharmed. Realising that the longer this animal was fought the more dangerous it would become, I signalled to the president to change the act. The trumpets sounded and my *banderilleros* prepared to place the darts.

Standing by the barrier waiting to take the sword and *muleta*, I watched the *cuadrilla* at work. As each pair of darts was placed the bull cut ground towards the man. It was obvious from the way it acted that it had been fought before at some stage of its life, probably by a boy who had sneaked out on to the ranch at night and fought it by moonlight in the open country. The thoughtlessness of my own action, when I had participated in such an escapade on the Gallardo ranch, was now being brought home to me with a vengeance and I was experiencing the way I might have jeopardised the lives of other *toreros*.

The only way this bull could be fought was "from horn to horn". Spreading the *muleta* over the sword and holding both in my right hand I ran out to a very short distance from his head and dropped to one knee—the knee nearest the horns. Then, holding the lure close to my body, I swung its furthest point towards the offside horn and, as the bull charged, I flopped it over his head from one horn to the other, thus bringing him to my opposite side, when I turned and dropped to the other knee. After repeating the process fourteen or fifteen times I managed to get the bull into a position for killing. This, I knew, was going to be tricky, so as I went in, I swept the *muleta* in my left hand wide across my body and outwards, trying to lead him well clear of my stomach; but instead of following the cloth and passing to my right the bull ran straight out to the left. Fortunately I was over the boss as he tossed upwards, but the flat of his right horn crashed sickeningly against my left knee. I staggered from the encounter and found that I could put no weight on my leg. The bull was mortally wounded and had no further interest in me so I tried to walk from the ring, but the pain was excruciating and my *banderilleros* had to carry me to the *enfermeria*. The knee was swollen to twice its normal size with the flesh across it split wide open. After sewing the gash, the surgeons put an elastic bandage on my knee and told me to go straight to the bullfighters' hospital on reaching Madrid.

Pepe managed to procure a walking stick for me and aided by this I was able to hobble down to the square in the evening where we sat drinking and watching the dancing and festivities until it was time for us to leave for Madrid.

The train pulled into the capital at seven o'clock in the morning, an early hour there, and we had to make our way around piles of fish boxes before finding a taxi. Driving along the *Paseo del Prado* which leads from *Atocha* station to the *Plaza de Cibeles* we noticed several people waving to us. We waved back. A little further along, we passed a tram and more people waved to us. Again we waved back. It is easy to identify the cars in which bullfighters are travelling to or from a *corrida* by the *espuerta*, the leather box which holds the costume, capes and *muletas* and which is invariably carried on the roof of the car. It can be pleasing to be recognised and acclaimed and on this occasion I was proud that Jacqueline was there to share it with me. Feeling regal, I returned their salutations, but suddenly I received a shock, for looking out of the window I realised that our offside rear wheel was bowling along beside us, happy to be free from the rest of the car. No wonder everyone had waved so frantically; they were trying to attract our attention to the impending disaster.

Yelling to the driver that we were a wheel short, I threw my weight on to the near side of the cab. We pulled into the side of the road still upright on three wheels, the escaped wheel continuing its journey unimpeded. The driver was profuse in his apologies for the incident and absolutely refused to allow me to pay him for the part of the journey we had already covered. He hailed another taxi and transferred the luggage. We arrived at our respective homes without further incident.

Breakfasted and changed, I first went to my barber's to be shaved and then on to the bullfighters' hospital which is close to the bullring. My knee was thoroughly examined and the verdict was that the patella was undoubtedly cracked. The only cure was to keep the elastic bandage on and my weight off my leg as much as possible. One thing was certain. It would be a long job and meant definitely no more bull-fighting for the rest of the season. What shattering news! Only three *corridas* that year and each one had culminated in injury. Now I was finished until the following spring.

Not being able to get about very much, I spent the best part of my time sitting in the café with my manager and several bullfight enthusiasts. Jacqueline sometimes came with me and strangely enough she was immediately accepted by this circle which by tradition was strictly male. It was surprising to hear the *aficionados* discussing bullfighting with her and asking for her opinion on various taurine matters.

We never missed an opportunity of watching the twice weekly *corridas* and Jacqueline's knowledge and appreciation of the art was greatly increased by these practical studies. I used to ask her to estimate the bulls as soon as they entered the ring and whilst the *banderilleros* were doing the pre-liminary capework. In a very short time she became an excellent judge and could tell me how each *matador* should handle individual animals.

Madrid at this time was full of tourists and usually we found ourselves sitting within earshot of some of them. It was interesting to note the reactions of our compatriots watching their first bullfights. Surprisingly enough we discovered that the women generally took immediately to the *fiesta* whilst the men would often get up and leave after the first fight. Generally speaking, the younger people stood up to it less well than the middle-aged and elderly.

One very distinct memory was of two very aged people whom we judged to be in their late seventies. They were sitting immediately behind us and watched the whole of the *corrida* through a pair of field-glasses which they kept passing backwards and forwards to each other. Through their remarks about various aspects of the fight, it was obvious that they were thoroughly enjoying the whole spectacle and did not intend to miss a thing. During the *pic*-ing of the fifth bull, one of the rare accidents to the horses occurred. The bull had charged the horse and pushed it round, so that, before the *picador* could do anything to protect his mount, the latter had its unprotected flank ripped open. There was an immediate cascade of viscera.

Anxious for our two aged neighbours, I half turned in my seat to see how they had taken this unpleasant sight. The old lady was passing the glasses over to the old man and I was staggered to hear her say. "Have a look, William, you can see everything—its liver and intestines and all."

As always in such cases, the horse was speedily slaughtered on the spot by one of the bullring attendants. The old lady remained quite unmoved by the sight of the destruction of this noble animal.

Quite often we were amused by the know-all types who would keep up running commentaries to their companions during the fights, and it was enlightening to hear some of the many misconceptions people have about bullfighting. They believed that the bulls are doped before coming into the ring, that the horses have their vocal cords cut to prevent them screaming (a common occurrence in England, where racehorses' vocal cords are often painlessly cut in order to help them to breathe—this does not stop them from whinnying), that the bull closes its eyes when charging and that therefore it is easy for the *matador* not to be caught. I could fill a book with the ridiculous ideas some people hold about the *corrida*. One of the commonest, of course, is that the bull cannot tolerate the sight of red and for this reason it will repeatedly attack the *muleta*. I do not know whether bulls are colour blind or not and I cannot see how this can be proved one way or the other, but I am certain that they have no aggressive reaction to the colour red, for they will attack the yellow side of the fighting cape with as much vigour as they will the crimson side. I heard one man proclaiming in a loud voice that—"the poor beast is aggravated by that red rag". I couldn't stop myself from pointing out to him that one of the *toreros* was wearing a red costume and asked him why, in this case, the bull didn't attack the man instead of the cape. Of course he was lost for a reply.

Bullfighting is based on the theory of the bull being in perfect physical condition, meeting a man on foot, face to face, for the first time. If the bull is interfered with by doping or being punished before coming into the ring, as the opponents of the *fiesta* would have it, the sole result would be to endanger the *matador* to an even greater extent. A bull not in full possession of its faculties, either mental or physical, is unpredictable and an unpredictable bull is doubly dangerous.

Government regulations lay down the rules of bullfighting in all its aspects, controlling the actions of bullfighters, bull-breeders and promoters alike. In most bullrings, and certainly in all the major *plazas*, these regulations are strictly observed. The *mayoral*, or head cowboy, travels with the animals to the bullrings to assure the breeder that they are delivered safely and are not touched en-route. In the corrals of the bullring, if the *mayoral* does not continue to guard them, the job is handed over to a Civic Guard. Every precaution is taken to ensure that the beasts are not tampered with.

Until 1953 these precautions were not so rigidly enforced and many of the top *matadores* were paying to have their bulls *afeitado*, shaved, which meant that a few centimetres were cut from the tips of each horn. Quite often this made the points finer than they were originally, but the loss of these few centimetres was sufficient to make the bull misjudge his distance, though by no means make him harmless. It simply gave the *matador* a better chance of getting away with his life, should the bull catch him.

The action a bull uses in tossing is to ram the horn into the flesh, then to lift its head and toss. An old bull with plenty of experience of fighting on the ranges amongst the herd, has learned how to use its horns well. It will throw a man into the air with one horn and catch him on the other as he comes down, then continue to toss him between the two, four or five times before throwing him to the ground. Therefore the removal of this small piece of horn from the tips would tend to make a bull toss before coming into full contact with its adversary, and the cloth of the *torero's* costume would suffer in place of his flesh.

During my first season I witnessed an unforgettable occurrence. I was on a ranch in Andalucia selecting some bulls, and at the same time a *corrida* of six bulls was being enclosed and boxed prior to shipment to a bullring. Whenever possible I took the opportunity of watching the bulls run through the corrals where they were separated by a cleverly designed system of doors.

The sliding door of the box had been dropped behind the third bull when the *mayoral*, who knew me well, called me over to where he was standing beside the main corral.

"Vicente," he said, "something interesting is going on that I would like you to see."

Following in his wake, I walked round to the back of the corrals to where the box used as the bulls' hospital stood. A large black bull with fine curving horns was enclosed in the box and one of the cowboys was endeavouring to secure a rope about its horns.

"The barber's shop," commented the *mayoral*, indicating the scene before us. "They are 'shaving' one of the animals being sent off today," he continued, with obvious repugnance to the idea.

"I would never have believed that Don Fulano allowed this to happen to his bulls," I said, amazed at what I saw.

"It is the only way the *fenomenos* of today will accept bulls from this ranch. Our animals are too much for the modern stars of the ring," the *mayoral* stated with more than a touch of sarcasm in his voice. I knew that his dislike of bullfighters was only equalled by his love for the animals he reared.

"But a little bit off the horn can hardly hurt the animals?" I asked.

"Just watch and then tell me that," he answered.

By this time the rope had been secured and the bull's head was being twisted in such a manner that one horn was outside the box. Another rope was passed around the beast's neck and two of the ranch hands applied their full weight to it. The bull's eyes were wide with fear and rolling so that practically only the whites showed. Its breathing was laboured and it bellowed in bewilderment as it struggled against its bonds.

The ranch hands never relaxed their pressure for a moment as one of their number began sawing through the horn with a hacksaw about half an inch from the point. The severed portion fell to the ground and the man with the hacksaw replaced this tool with a rasp and started rasping the now blunt horn to a point. Having shaped it to his satisfaction he then filed out the rasp marks until the point was smooth again. The tip of the horn was then oiled to give it a shiny finish. Once the operation was completed, it was difficult to see the effects of the mutilation. The whole performance was then repeated on the other side, after which the bull was released into the corral, bellowing and trying to shake the strain out of its twisted neck. I was disgusted with what I had seen.

"Well?" The *mayoral* looked enquiringly at me. "What do you think of that?"

"It's shocking," I admitted. I felt sickened at the treatment the beast had received. Not so much from the cutting of the horns, which in this case I don't suppose caused it any more inconvenience than cutting a finger nail would inconvenience a human being. It was the method employed to perform the operation that appalled me, seeing such a noble creature so obviously terrified and bewildered. The word "bull" always conjures up a picture of well-armed magnificence, and the sight of one of these beasts, frightened and defenceless, nauseated me. I swore there and then that I would never fight bulls I knew to be "doctored" in this manner.

"Do many of the bulls receive this treatment?" I enquired.

"Most of them that go to major bullfights," came the reply.

"What about those going to Madrid and Sevilla?" I continued.

"They get the same treatment. If expertly done, it is very difficult to detect unless the horns are inspected at close range and as that can only be efficiently done after the animal is dead, nobody bothers."

In 1952, Antonio Bienvenida, one of Spain's finest *matadores* and one of the old school, denounced the practice of the *afeitado* to the press and a tremendous scandal resulted from his articles. The regulations were tightened up and it was made law that all bulls should be inspected after death and if this resulted in the discovery that their horns had been tampered with, a heavy fine and six months' suspension would be imposed on the person or persons responsible.

If the "shaving" had taken place on the ranch, then the bull-breeder was to be fined and suspended from sending bulls to the bullrings for a period of six months. The effects of this would be disastrous to the breeder concerned as he would miss most of the season, with the result that his bulls would be a year older by the following season and therefore more difficult to dispose of, apart from the cost of extra feed and maintenance. The effect on the bullfighter or bullfight promoter, if it was proved that the bulls had been interfered with since their arrival at the ring, would be equally disastrous both financially and from the point of view of prestige. I believe that the practice has been ended now, at least in Spain.

At the close of the 1951 season Jacqueline and I decided to winter in England. Although neither of us had spoken of marriage it was mutually assumed that that step would be the natural outcome of our friendship.

11

IN London the press were quick to notice our association and printed photographs of us together, labelling Jacqueline as "El Ingles's new fiancée, Jacqueline the second."

She took this in good part and it was one night after a Christmas party that I asked her to marry me. She agreed and we planned to return to Spain together and marry there.

Shortly after this, however, she was offered a job as correspondent on the Côte D'Azur for a publicity agency and I advised her to accept the post, postponing our marriage until the end of the season. I returned to Spain alone.

Arriving at the end of February, I went straight to the country to fight at the *tientas* and soon found myself in the peak of condition again, with no derogatory effects from my accidents of the previous year. I trained hard, for the season was to start well. My manager had already signed a number of contracts, the first one being for Easter Sunday. Practically every town in Spain holds a *corrida* on this day and bullfighters not contracted to appear somewhere can consider themselves to be in for a pretty bad season. In fact *toreros* who get few contracts are called "Easter Sunday" fighters, meaning that they only appear when bullfighters are in demand.

It is the dream of most small boys in Spain to become *toreros* and a large number retain their aspirations in their youth, but many fall by the wayside, either after their first contact with an animal or, if they stand up to this test, after their first goring. In many cases their valour seeps away with their blood. Nevertheless, the competition amongst *toreros* is very great and, apart from the lucky few, there are hundreds who try to scrape a living every year. You will see them in their dozens, sitting in the cafés frequented by the profession. Always well-dressed, they sit there day after day, telling each other of the big contracts that are just around the corner. Sometimes they will disappear for a day or two to fight in some remote village for just their expenses, then reappear to tell everyone willing to listen of the great triumphs they have produced. It is incredible the way they exist with only sufficient money in their pockets to pay for the one coffee which lasts them most of the day.

The courage the majority of these lads display in front of the bulls is enormous but very few have the courage to admit to themselves that they are wasting their lives waiting for the "something" that will never come. An exception to this rule, however, was a friend of mine from Valencia. I will call him Valenciano.

All his life Valenciano had dreamed of becoming one of the hallowed stars of the ring and, along with the other boys of his age who shared his dreams, he trained assiduously every day in the bullring of Valencia. After several years of practice he fought at one or two *tientas*; then at last came his big opportunity. He was given a chance to appear in a novices' fight. Six bulls for six *matadores*, with a contract for a regular fight to the two boys who showed most promise. The great day arrived and Valenciano, in his hired costume, took his place amongst the other aspirants. When his turn came, the bull was loosed and his *banderilleros* did the preliminary running before signalling him to move in. He did so, and after the first two passes decided there and then that the vocation of the ring was not for him. So, folding his cape, he strode across the sand to retire behind the barrier. Of course the reaction of the public was as might be expected; they threw everything within their reach at him, but although they slanged him, Valenciano had the courage of his convictions and remained behind the safety of the fence. He knew that he could, and probably would, be gaoled for this action, or rather lack of action, but he remained firm. After all, having taken the decision not to become a *torero*, why risk his life with this bull? Subsequently he was gaoled for twenty-four hours and, when released, fulfilled his avowed intentions of finding himself another, more placid, occupation by taking employment as a shop assistant and has never to this day had any more thoughts of donning the silk and gold.

Another friend who soon decided not to pursue his hopes of glory after his first fight was Nick Allen, an ex-R.A.F. man and ex-pupil of Gordonstoun, who after reading in the press about my performances decided that he would do likewise. He made his debut in La Linea but after the fight, resigned himself to a less adventurous life teaching English in Madrid.

A surprising number of boys write to me stating that they would like to become *matadores*; even a few girls have had the same idea, but I try to explain the dangers and difficulties before telling them they would be better off in a safer profession. One boy who remained undaunted by all the pitfalls I pointed out to him, was Geoffrey Keat from Laindon in Essex. Geoffrey was set on this ambition and for a year I gave him lessons in the basic principles of *tauromaquia*. He proved to be a very apt pupil and learned quickly. He is now in Spain training and has already fought in a few *tientas*. I won't forecast that he'll become a *torero* as I haven't seen him perform with an animal, but he had great possibilities.

Although bullfighting is so wholly Spanish, I do not believe that this should prevent non-Spaniards from succeeding in it. One quality which most of the greatest *matadores* have possessed is the ability to act calmly and think quickly and clearly in moments of extreme crisis; a characteristic supposedly typical of the more phlegmatic Anglo-Saxons. The theory of the art is easily learned and the ability to perform the various passes soon accomplished. Where the Spaniard has the great advantage is in his inborn aesthetic appreciation and aptitude. His grace is natural to him and forms part of his complex make-up.

It was this "putting feeling into my work" that I found most difficult. In my first fights, do what I would with the bulls, I knew that there was always something important lacking. I couldn't pinpoint it and it took a bout of fever to show me what it was.

The fight in which this realisation came to me took place in a little town named Ubrique, in the province of Ronda. It was a relatively unimportant fight and on the day previous to it my temperature had risen to 102° F., so I telephoned the impresario to cancel my contract. He was terribly disappointed and pleaded so strongly that I relented, and thinking that by the morrow the fever, a common condition in the south, would have abated, I promised to appear. However, my temperature didn't drop and owing to the way I felt on arrival at the bullring, I decided that I wouldn't attempt too much but just get through with a bare minimum.

By the time my first bull came in, the fever in me raged high. I completed a couple of *veronicas*, then I heard one of the spectators jeering that I was fighting too far away from the horns. What happened after that I am not quite sure, but after killing the bull I remember that there was a thunderous burst of applause and the president awarded me the two ears, tail and a hoof.

Later, back at the hotel, I tried to analyse my actions, but for the first time I was unable to. Previously I had always been able to re-enact each *faena* pass by pass. What in fact had occurred was that through being provoked I had completely let myself go and not planned each move before making it. I had let inspiration take over from calculated action.

A reminder of this incident came in my first fight of the 1952 season. For some unknown reason I had not been able to settle down with my first bull and my *quites* had not brought any reaction from the public. I took the *muleta* and sword and began a *faena* of right-handed passes but still the audience remained unresponsive, apart from a little polite applause. I was giving a stereotyped performance and knew it. Then the bull caught me and sent me spinning. It acted like a spur and, as in Ubrique, I began fighting without planning. The effect on the public was immediate and the intoxication of the situation took control of my movements. The result of the fight was an enormous success.

Alejandro was kept busy signing contracts and the *cuadrilla* and I travelled ceaselessly, fighting in all parts of the Peninsula. The travelling is very tiring and sometimes in the height of the season we would leave one ring, pile into the car, and drive all night to arrive at our destination with barely enough time to change our clothes. Once or twice we didn't even have time for this and travelled in our costumes.

The preoccupation with so much fighting left me little time to think of anything else but bulls, though usually I found time to telephone Jacqueline in Cannes and tell her the results of the day's *corrida*.

One fight that remains in my memory, not so much from the actual *corrida* but from the incidents appertaining to it, was at Tolosa, a Basque town near San Sebastian.

It was arranged that we should make the journey in the car of a friend of mine named Jones, who worked in the British Embassy in Madrid. My manager was to travel with us and also another Englishman resident in Madrid, named Tommy Morrison. Tommy and I were very good friends and though it had long been his wish to see me fight, he had never before had the time to spare from his business to travel with me. I promised to dedicate one of the bulls to him.

Setting off from Madrid the evening before the day of the *orrida*, we travelled all through the night and whilst Jones drove the long distance, the rest of us slept peacefully in the spacious car. It was 7.30 a.m. when we arrived in Tolosa and we made straight for the hotel so that we might bathe and change before breakfast.

On entering the hotel we were astonished to find the place apparently deserted. Ascending the stairs we tried the bathrooms but they were without hot water, so once again we searched the ground floor for signs of life, but still there was no one to be seen. Tommy suggested that we should drive into San Sebastian and breakfast there. We left the hotel quite unmolested and as far as we could see, quite at liberty to ransack the place.

Bathed and refreshed, we breakfasted in the hotel dining room which overlooked San Sebastian's uniquely beautiful bay of "La Concha". It was still early and the returning anchovy boats were coming alongside and tying up in the tiny harbour. We walked round the bay to watch them unload their silvery contents as the dealers bid in competition to secure the overflowing boxes of fish.

Alejandro suggested that we should kill time before returning to Tolosa for the *sorteo* by visiting the aquarium for which San Sebastian is renowned. Being a keen fisherman, I'm fascinated by aquariums and could spend hours watching the fishes glide to and fro in their tanks. One of the keepers amused us by holding a lighted match in front of the glass of the tank containing the octopi. These weird creatures, attracted by the light, wafted through the water with a waltzing movement of their tentacles and endeavoured to grasp the flame in their nauseating mouths.

I terrified my manager by showing him the sea snakes. Bullfighters are terribly superstitious about snakes and believe them to be portenders of the direst evil. Alejandro's belief in the superstition was so great that he would not even pronounce the word *serpiente* and when, of necessity, he had to mention them, would refer to them as "those things". Once he refused to speak to Jacqueline for several days when she had teasingly threatened to bring one to him after he had suggested arranging for me a *corrida* of *Miuras*—a breed of bulls which have caused more deaths among bullfighters than any other. On another occasion when Jacqueline, wearing a pair of snakeskin shoes, had accompanied me to a café used by *toreros*, those present had been frightened out of the place by the mere sight of her footwear.

The contents of the aquarium held our interest to such an extent that the fight was almost forgotten and we had to rush madly back to Tolosa for the *sorteo*. The other *toreros* had been waiting quite a time for us, so we dared not excuse ourselves by saying that fishes had kept us from bulls.

The bulls were small and I was pleased with the pair that I drew. The first, a dark grey, turned out to be exceptionally good.

Whilst I was resting before the *corrida*, the locals were entertaining Tommy and Jones on a great scale, and by the time of the fight Tommy was a little more than happy.

Out of deference to the public of Tolosa, I dedicated my first bull, the grey, to them. I began my *faena* with the *muleta* by doing six passes close to the barrier with both knees on the ground, and then continued with right and left-handed passes of every description. After three *molinetes*, in which I dropped to my knees spinning between the horns, I attempted a right-handed chest pass on one knee but misjudging the distance, I was caught and tossed, fortunately without serious consequences. I killed the bull with the first swordthrust and was awarded the two ears and a tail.

My second bull was the one I intended to dedicate to my friend Tommy and at the sound of the trumpet signal for the

(*Right*) A *media veronica* in Madrid. (*Below*) A few minutes later this happened. (*Photo: Martin.*)

(*Above*) Taking a heavy toss in the Madrid bullring. (*Photo: Martin Santos Yuberg*.) (*Right*) With the ears of the last bull I killed at a charity fight in La Linea, wearing *traje corto*. (*Photo: Russell Westwood*.)

banderilleros to clear the ring, I took the sword and *muleta* and, with my hat in my right hand, went to where Tommy was sitting in the front row. Arriving before him, I raised my hat and pronounced the dedication. Tommy rose in his seat to acknowledge it but as I tossed up my hat to him, he stumbled and fell into the lap of the woman sitting next to him. The audience thought this involuntary clowning a wonderful spectacle and roared with laughter, but the woman concerned was most indignant about it. After I had finished my *faenas* and despatched the bull, I returned to claim my hat from Tommy but he was not ready for me and had to hunt around on the ground between his feet where he had dropped it. I liked Tommy too much to be annoyed, but a dedication is supposed to be a serious affair.

Amongst their most popular diversions, the Basques rate eating and drinking highly. The size of the meals they consume has to be witnessed to be believed. They even have eating clubs, each member having a key to the clubroom where at any time of the day or night he can cook a meal. They are also great cider drinkers and inter-town and inter-province contests are held every year.

One of these clubs had arranged a banquet in my honour and with typical Spanish hospitality, invited Tommy and Jones to join us. Alejandro, of course, was also a guest.

At the banquet there were very few speeches as these were considered to interfere with the more important task of eating. Course after course appeared and as soon as I managed to finish one dish another would take its place. All this delicious food was washed down with prodigious quantities of local wine.

It was during coffee that the subject of cider was raised and I discovered that seated next to me was the champion cider drinker of Guipuzcoa, the province in which Tolosa is situated. He was enumerating the qualities of Guipuzcoan cider when I said to him:

"The cider you drink here is nothing to its English counterpart, especially that which comes from the county of Devon."

"Have you ever drunk our cider?" blustered the champion.

"Yes, and I find it weak and flat," I answered truthfully, knowing that this would provoke him.

"Weak?" he almost bellowed.

"I was weaned on stronger stuff," I taunted.

The others seated nearby were enjoying seeing their champion enraged. Then the inevitable challenge came.

"I defy you to drink with me," he pronounced.

"I accept," I replied.

My contestor clapped his hands and yelled for bottles.

We started drinking and at first the champion drew ahead, but I doggedly plodded along behind him until I was fit to burst. Eventually I had to ask him if I might leave the table for a brief moment.

"It is not really allowed during a contest, but perhaps just this once . . . " he conceded.

I quickly went to the lavatory. Maybe this wasn't exactly playing the game but I didn't possess the capacity of my bulky challenger.

We continued the contest and soon the champion began to flag and I gained on him. Eventually he could take no more and I outdrank him by a few glasses. He was incredulous and crestfallen at my success.

The banquet over, we all repaired to the village square where a dance was in progress. We passed the night dancing and singing until it was suggested that we should have one for the road at the "Club Mercantil".

It was three-thirty a.m. when I opened the door of my room and found Tommy fast asleep in my bed. During the course of the evening's festivities I had lost sight of Tommy, Alejandro, and Jones. Now I had found one of the trio, and being in dire need of a good sleep myself I was too tired to worry over the whereabouts of the other two. I made myself as comfortable as possible on the room's second bed which possessed the scanty covering of a thin quilt.

Hardly had I settled beneath this when in walked Jones, stating that *he* was ready to start for Madrid. Tommy was still asleep and as it was as much as I could do to keep my eyes open, I told him to go on without us, that we could easily catch a train or hire a car in the morning, and immediately I fell asleep.

It was daylight when I was awakened by the sound of animated conversation. Opening my eyes I looked at my watch which showed the time to be only six-thirty a.m. Looking up I saw Tommy on the balcony talking to someone in the street. I hurried over to see what was going on and looking down I saw Jones standing there. Apparently he had driven about twenty kilometres, then thinking better of his desertion had returned for us, but added that if we didn't hurry he was going to leave again.

Dressing rapidly, we packed and raced downstairs into the car and set off for Madrid. After driving for two hours, Jones, who had not had a wink of sleep for over forty-eight hours, decided that he could go no further without resting, so pulling into the side of the road he dozed off. Tommy and I got out of the car and stretched our legs.

"I'd give anything for a drink," said Tommy.

"So would I," I agreed. "My mouth feels as if it's lined with mink."

About a mile down the road we could see a farmhouse which was the only dwelling in sight and, in fact, the first we had seen for some time, as this rugged part of the country is very sparsely populated.

"Let's walk down there and see if they have any wine," suggested Tommy, indicating the distant building.

"There's not a hope," I replied. "Although we'll probably be able to get some milk there."

"I've a feeling we'll find something better than that," insisted my friend.

Together we set off down the road in the direction of the lone farmhouse. It was a long, low building and I was surprised to see the number 19 painted on the front door. From the number of houses we had passed en-route so far, I calculated that numbers 18 and 20 would be about two miles away. We knocked on the door and the sound reverberated through the house. We knocked again but there was no reply. Suddenly we heard a voice behind us and turning, saw a little girl of about twelve years of age.

"What is it that you want?" she enquired politely.

"We wondered if you have anything to drink," I replied.

Excusing herself, the little girl pushed past us and opening the door of the house, stood inside the doorway and bid us follow. As we entered several chickens ran clucking away from almost under our feet. Looking to my right I saw what I supposed was the living room. On the floor was a heap of fodder and in the corner, a tiny, long-legged black piglet was snuffling. We followed the girl through another door and into a narrow stone-floored room. We could hardly believe our eyes when we entered the room. It was fully equipped as a bar. A high counter of scrubbed wood divided off a third of the room and behind this was arranged a wonderful stock of bottles.

The little girl slipped behind the counter and with a very professional air asked, "What will the gentlemen take?"

"Is it too much to ask for some beer?" I asked hopefully.

"We have some here keeping cool," she said, and pointed to a large earthenware bowl half-filled with water and containing a dozen bottles of "El Aguila" beer.

"If you will wait a moment, I will get some clean glasses," said the child.

"Don't worry about that," I told her. "We'll have all those just as they are."

Between us, Tommy and I carried the earthenware bowl containing the bottles out on to the roadside. I always carried on me a combined corkscrew and bottle-opener and with this handy tool we opened a couple of bottles and drained them down our parched throats. We had been sitting there for over an hour marvelling at this oasis when Jones appeared with the car, and we continued our journey.

It was seven-thirty p.m. when we eventually drew up outside Tommy's house. He had suggested that I joined him for dinner and that we should spend the evening continuing our celebrations. I wasn't due to appear in the ring again for a fortnight so I readily agreed to this suggestion.

Whilst Tommy searched for his latch-key, I began unloading the luggage from the boot of the car. First there was my small suitcase, then the *espuerta*, followed by two other cases which I took to be Tommy's. Tommy, however, only claimed one of these. I asked Jones if the other was his, to which he replied that he had his stuff inside the car with him. It was then that the terrible truth dawned upon me. The odd bag out belonged to my manager and we had come away without him.

My swordhandler had collected the money after the fight and after paying the *cuadrilla*, had handed the balance to me. In our haste, we had left without paying the hotel bill and I was pretty certain that Alejandro did not have enough cash with him to settle it. I immediately telephoned his wife, a level-headed Basque woman, and spent a long time trying to convince her that we really had forgotten him and that he had not been arrested, a secret though inexplicable fear of hers every time her husband travelled away from home.

Two days later my manager arrived. The morning after the fight he had woken to find that we had left the hotel without trace. He had had to borrow money to pay the bill and buy himself a train ticket. To add to his chagrin, there had been no seats available on the express that day and his only alternative was to journey on the slow mail train. When I met him at the station he had been travelling for fourteen hours and was in a somewhat irritable frame of mind, but being an *Andaluz*, he was quick to forgive and forget.

My last formal *corrida* of the season was at Barcelona, the great rambling industrial port and busy metropolis of Cataluña whose surrounding coastline was of exquisite beauty. I always enjoyed my visits there and especially this time, as the fight was in honour of the British Fleet which was in port.

Shortly after my return to Madrid, Jacqueline arrived from Cannes. The season there had closed and she wanted to spend a few weeks in Spain before returning to England. Earlier in the summer I had promised to appear in a charity fight at La Linea, for the benefit of the orphans of the soldiers of the Spanish Southern Command. This was to take place on the first Sunday in October so I didn't have to leave for a week or two, but decided that immediately after the fight, on returning to London, I would marry Jacqueline.

Together with Alejandro I travelled down to La Linea on the night express and as we sat in our sleeper I was reminded of the night four years previously when I had made this identical trip for the first time. So much had happened since then; far more than I had hoped for or even thought possible. At the time I had not really believed that I would actually become a *torero*. My hopes and dreams had seemed so far away and unattainable.

I was as excited as a schoolboy at the thought of returning to La Linea once again. I had seen my first bullfight there, had had my presentation as a professional *torero* there, and I knew that if I married now, this would be my last fight there.

As the train thundered on through the night I reflected on the events of the past few years. Somehow it still seemed unbelievable. I had to look up at the *espuerta* containing my capes and *muletas* and the tooled leather case which held my set of matched swords nestling in the luggage rack, in order to convince myself that the whole thing had been reality and not a dream. As I lay in my bunk, swaying gently to the motions of the train, my fingers ran over the scars on my legs. They were real enough. I realised that I had been very lucky to get away as lightly as I had.

Many of my companions had fared far worse. I still had my health and strength whilst several of them were sick and broken. They have a saying in Spain, *Los toros dan pero tambien quitan*—The bulls give but they also take away. Maybe it would be better to retire from the ring when I married and whilst I was in one piece.

The train drew on to the quayside at Algeciras almost on time and Pedro was there to greet us and take charge of the luggage. In order to save the organisers of the charity fight unnecessary expense I had left my *cuadrilla* behind and intended to use local *banderilleros*—there were to be no *picadores*. I had previously telephoned Pedro asking him to book the *banderilleros* who had formed part of my *cuadrilla* on the day of my debut.

It was wonderful to see my old swordhandler again and we had a lot to talk about as we took a glass of wine before he stowed the luggage into the car that was taking my manager and me to La Linea. We had reserved accommodation at the "Hotel Universal" where it had been arranged that I should have the same suite in which I had spent so much time after my first goring.

Although only two years had passed since I had last been there, La Linea seemed to have changed, even in that short time. One of the most striking sights was the American sailors who thronged every bar in town. Their Mediterranean Fleet was in Gibraltar and for the first time, due to the American–Spanish pact, the sailors were allowed across the frontier in uniform.

I purposely waited until evening before seeing Adolfo Beaty, so it was not until after dinner that I strolled down to the *Club Mercantil*. As on that first evening when Adolfo had introduced me to the circle, all my friends were seated on the wicker chairs outside the club, all of them that is except *El Mosquito*, and, as before, his grotesquely distorted chair remained empty awaiting his arrival. We sat talking until the early hours.

The next morning Alejandro and I went down to the bullring to take a look at the bulls and watch them being penned. As the six bulls came from different ranches, there was no *sorteo*. The six *matadores*, according to their seniority, would take the bulls according to the antiquity of the herd from which they came. I was second in seniority and it fell to me to kill a red two-year-old from Juan Gallardo's ranch, his herd being the second oldest.

Whilst we were at the bullring, Sidney Franklin, the American *ex-torero*, appeared. He suggested that we should organise a formal *corrida* for the following Sunday so that we could take advantage of the presence of the American sailors. I told him that I would decide later and let him know.

In charity fights the *toreros* taking part do not dress in the customary silk costume but wear *traje corto*, the suit worn at the *tientas*. These clothes are comparatively easy to don and as I could dress practically unaided, Pedro, who was handling my swords for me, did not come to the hotel until about half an hour before the fight was due to commence.

The drive to the bullring on this occasion was much shorter than on the day of my first fight, when I had dressed in Miguel's house; nevertheless I experienced the same pleasure as we drove through the milling crowds and people turned to wave and shout a welcome greeting.

Inside the bullring the scene was one I had witnessed time and time again but which never failed to thrill me; the mules restless in their jingling harness, the bustling of the officials and bullring attendants, the butchers preparing their tools and the quick view, through the half-open door of the *enfermeria*, of the surgeon and his assistants preparing the instruments in case they should be needed.

Walking through the tunnel of the *patio de cuadrillas*, I could see that every seat in the ring was occupied and the crowd was clearly impatient for the parade to start. As I appeared in the entrance a number of them spotted me and immediately, at the tops of their voices, began wishing me luck. Many of them called out, welcoming me back to what they termed as "my" bullring. I felt a great pride in the fact that I should be so remembered and so affectionately greeted.

Shortly after my arrival, Miguel Campos entered the ring with Adolfo Beaty. Miguel and I embraced each other and exchanged warm greetings. I had always liked him for he had helped me a great deal when I had first arrived in Spain. Adolfo was bursting with pleasure as the box-office had sold out hours previously.

"The only time we see the ring as full as this is when you are billed to appear here," he said to me.

I smiled, pleased with this acknowledgement from an impresario.

"Why haven't you booked me here more often then?" I asked.

"It hasn't been my fault, Vicente," replied Adolfo, trying to assure me. "The others in the syndicate said that you asked too much money."

"But you have just admitted that I always fill the ring. Surely that entitled me to ask a high price?"

"That is exactly what I told them, but they would not listen. Today has proved me right though," he said triumphantly. "We'll see you here more often in the future, I can assure you."

I didn't tell him that this would probably be my last appearance in any *Plaza de Toros*.

Across the ring we could see the president taking his place in the presidential box and, forming up with our *cuadrillas* behind us, we awaited the signal to parade. Dress capes are not worn with the *traje corto* but in their place a fighting cape is carried, folded across the left forearm. I was adjusting my cape when at last the trumpet sounded and we stepped forward. I led my *cuadrilla* across the ring, feeling sad as I did so. To me the parade had always been a wonderful moment. The fear gone, the tension broken and the public waiting. Now I wondered how I would be able to leave it all.

As there were no *picadores* being used we did not alternate in *quites* but remained behind the barrier until our particular bull was in the ring, though we were always in readiness to rush out should anybody be caught.

The door to the pens swung open for the second time and my bull trotted into the ring. As I had suspected, the beast did not turn out to be very good. The bulls used in charity fights are usually given by the breeders and are, more often than not, half-breeds or throw-outs from the main herd, so nothing very much is expected of them.

Each time I confronted the red bull with the cape, it backed away and I soon realised that the only way I could hope to get it to attack would be to back away myself and re-approach the horns again, cutting across what would be the animal's line of charge. By dint of patience and repeatedly retreating and advancing, I managed to make it attack and I passed it twice with *veronicas*. Then, not wishing to disillusion the animal too much, I asked the president to signal for the *banderillas* to be placed.

The bull bucked under the smart of the darts, trying to throw the paper-covered sticks from its shoulders. I took the *muleta* and sword, then waited until the bucking had ceased before advancing towards the animal. By placing my body close to the horns and giving the bull confidence that it had something solid to charge at, I managed to give it three right-handed passes, then, edging towards it to initiate the fourth pass, I swept the *muleta* up to almost the horn tips and shook it, calling to the bull as I did so. The animal turned tail and fled until one of my *banderilleros* ran out from the barrier and cut short its flight.

Time and time again I attempted to make it charge but to no avail. The only way left in which to square it up for the kill was to fight it "horn to horn". Dropping to one knee, I managed to execute sufficient of these half passes to chop the beast into a position to kill. Eager to make this swordthrust, perhaps the last I would ever make, as perfect as possible I took my time and carefully lined the bull up. Holding the *muleta* low in front of me I shuffled first to one side and then to the other, gently shaking it as I did so in order to keep the animal's attention fixed on it.

As I moved the bull moved too, shifting the position of its forelegs in order to follow my movements. Then, seeing that its hoofs were in line, I slowly raised the sword and sighted along its channelled blade, all the time keeping the *muleta* gently swaying in order not to lose the animal's attention for one instant. When I was sure that the bull's eyes were following the cloth I went in as slowly and as straight as possible. The blade of the sword disappeared as if inch by inch into the hide between the shoulder blades. For a moment the bull and I became united in one dramatic piece; then the form broke up. The bull had charged past and now stood facing me. The finger guard of the sword was pressed hard against the chestnut hair of its shoulders and a dark rivulet of blood sprang from beneath it to force a winding course down its foreleg and into the sand. The animal looked perplexed and then suddenly the glaze of death filled its eyes. It shuddered slightly, then its legs collapsed and it lay dead at my feet.

For a moment I stood looking down at the carcase from

which I had just removed life. I felt neither pride nor remorse, but only a great awareness of death and the utter finality it brings to all that we comprehend.

The crowd was cheering wildly as I turned and walked back towards the barrier and, looking up, I saw that many were waving white handkerchiefs, petitioning the president to award me the ears. I held out my hand for Pedro to pass me the towel and as I was wiping the blood from my fingers, Fernando, my old *banderillero*, handed me the two hairy red triangles as evidence of presidential approval.

The applause of the crowd was life-blood to me and I opened my heart to receive it. It was my public and they were cheering me. We had given each other all we could and the bond between us was strong. I had difficulty in keeping the tears from my eyes as I stood out there in the centre of the ring, bowing my appreciation for their support.

As I left the Plaza after the fight, it was with a heavy heart, and I became acutely conscious of my surroundings. Every smell associated with the sanded arena became a memory to be cherished and every horn score in its walls part of the picture that I should remember with such pleasant recollection.

Undressing in my hotel room, the usual flow of wellwishers who appear only when one has had a good day, called to offer their congratulations and I allowed myself to bathe in the flood of their admiration. Purposefully I didn't tell myself that if things had gone wrong I would have been left to change my clothes in depressing solitude. Instead, I took full advantage of this last opportunity to revel in the glory.

Faithful to my resolution, I returned to England, and Jacqueline and I were married. I have never been to a bullring since but the call is great, sometimes almost unbearable. The sound of a *pasodoble* makes my feet long to tread again the scorching sands. The smell of cattle brings nostalgic memories and a strong desire to face a bull alone once more.

GLOSSARY

AFEITADO. Shaved. In bullfighting circles it refers to the now prohibited practice of shaving a few centimetres from the tips of the bulls' horns.

AFICION. Love of bullfighting. The ardent fans are known as *aficionados*. The bull-ring public consists of *aficionados* and *espectadores*; the latter merely go to enjoy the spectacle.

AGUA. Water. Synonym for rain.

ALEGRIA. Happiness. A light-hearted *flamenco* song.

ALGUACILES. Or *alguacilillos*. Dressed in the costumes associated with the reign of Felipe II, these men act as liaison between the president of the fight and the bullfighters, ensuring that the president's orders are carried out. If any trophies are awarded to the *matadores* it is the *alguacilillo* who hands them to the *torero*.

AL QUARTEO and AL QUIEBRO. Methods of placing the *banderillas* explained in the text.

AMBIENTE. Atmosphere. *Ambiente Taurino* is to be found in the bars and cafés where bullfighters and their hangers-on meet to discuss "the bulls".

ARENEROS. Bullring servants whose job it is to see that the sand of the ring is in a fit condition for the *toreros* to fight upon. In between bulls, they smooth the surface of the ground and remove any dung dropped by the animals.

ASPIRANTE. Aspirant bullfighter. An *aspirante* must appear in ten fights before he is granted a union card.

BANDERILLERO. Assistant or *peon* who serves the *matador* on foot. It is the job of the *banderillero* to do the preliminary running of the bull to allow the *matador* to estimate his adversary. In the second act of the bullfight he places the *banderillas* or darts in the bull's shoulders. Each *matador* employs three *banderilleros*, one of whom is known as *banderillero de confianza*, usually an older man in whom the *matador* has particular confidence and who may advise the *matador* on the condition of the bulls.

BICHOS. Small insects. An affectionate or sometimes derogatory synonym for the bulls. A good bull is *un buen bicho* and a bad bull *un mal bicho*.

BODEGAS. Wine-cellars.

BURLADERO. A shelter of wooden planking which stands out about eighteen inches from the barrier of the bullring. The space behind is wide enough to admit a man but too narrow for the bull. Most bullrings have four *burladeros* and each covers a space in the barrier through which the bullfighters may move from the arena into the *callejon*, the narrow corridor running between arena and spectators. In bullrings which have no barrier and *callejon* there will be several *burladeros*, to accommodate swordhandlers, doctors, etc.

CABALLOS. Horses. *Patio de caballos*, the courtyard in which the *picadores'* horses are saddled and harnessed into their protective padding. This is where the *picadores* wait before the parade begins.

CABALLERO. Gentleman. There are many of these in Spain.

CALLEJON. The corridor that runs between the arena and the spectators in which the bullfighters stand when not in action. Here too the swordhandlers, managers, doctors and bullring servants stand. It also usually contains an assortment of people who have no right to be there and whose sole purpose appears to be to hamper those who should.

CAPITALISTA. See *Espontaneo*.

CARRETON. A device used by bullfighters in practice. It consists of a pair of horns or an entire bull's head mounted on a bicycle wheel and is pushed by means of handles, like a barrow.

CHICO. Young boy.

COMISARIO. Chief of Police.

CORNADA. A deep and serious horn wound.

CORRIDA. The Spanish term for the bullfight. Literally it means running. Thus, a *corrida de toros* is a "running of mature bulls" and a *corrida de novillos-toros* is a "running of immature or defective bulls".

CRIADILLAS. The testicles of a dead bull. They are a delicacy and are usually served sliced and fried.

CUADRILLA. The *matador's* team of assistants containing three *banderilleros*, two *picadores* and one swordhandler.

DESCABELLO. The act of severing the bull's spinal cord between the skull and first vertebra which causes the bull to die immediately. This is employed after the swordthrust between the shoulder-blades has failed to drop the bull quickly.

DIA DE LOS REYES. The day of Kings which falls on the sixth of January or Twelfth Night.

ENFERMERIA. The operating theatre which is attached to every bullring.

ESPONTANEO. Usually young boys who wish to become bullfighters and in order to attract attention to themselves, jump into the bullring during the course of the fight and attempt to make passes with the bull. From the fact that they try to capitalise with someone else's bull, they are also called *capitalistas*. The punishment received by *espontaneos* is fifteen days in jail and prohibition from attending bullfights for a year.

ESPUERTA. The leather box in which a *matador's* equipment is carried.

ESTOCADA. The swordthrust made between the bull's shoulder-blades and which, if correctly placed, should cut the aorta. If only half the sword enters it is called a *media estocada*.

FAENA. In the bullring, *faena* means a series of passes which is entire within itself. A *matador* endeavours to create several *faenas* during the preparation for the final swordthrust. On the ranches where the bulls are bred, all acts such as the *tientas*, branding, herding and boxing of the bulls are called *faenas del campo*.

FENOMINOS. Phenomena. Nearly all young bullfighters are described as being *fenominos*. Apart from *dinero* (money) it is the favourite word of managers and promoters.

FIESTA. Party, holiday or carnival. The bullfight is known in Spain as *La fiesta nacional*.

FLAMENCO. Originally, pertaining to the gypsies. Nowadays used to describe the folklore of Andalucia. A typical Andalucian is described as being *muy flamenco* or very *flamenco*.

FRONTON. The courts where *pelota* is played. Often the game itself is referred to as *fronton*.

GUARDIA CIVIL. Civil Guards who are usually very uncivil. They are the armed national police of Spain and may easily be recognised by their Napoleonic hats.

JEFE. Chief. The *cuadrilla* call the *matador* "*Jefe*".

LA MACARENA. The *Virgen* of *La Macarena* is the Madonna of a church in Sevilla. She is held in great respect by bullfighters.

LEVANTE. A powerful east wind which blows on the coast of southern Spain.

MADRILEÑO. Native of Madrid.

MATADOR. Literally, killer. The *matador* is the star of the bullfight.

MAYORAL. Head cowboy. He tends the bulls during their lives and generally accompanies them to the bullring.

MEDIA. Half. *Medias* are stockings.

MELONCILLOS. Gray mongooses of the African species and which abound in the south of Spain.

MONTERA. The hat worn by *matadores* and *banderilleros*.

MULETA. A heart-shaped piece of red serge which is folded in half lengthwise and held on a stick by means of a spike at the far end and a thumbscrew at the near end. It is used by the *matador* during the third and final act of the bullfight.

NOCHE BUENA. The night of Christmas Eve.

NOTA. Note. A bull with a good *nota* carries good reports in the herd book.

PASE. Pass, either with the cape or *muleta*. The principal *pases* with the cape are the *veronica, chicuelina* and *gaonera* and with the *muleta, pase de la muerte, natural pase de pecho, molinetes, derechazos* and *manoletinas. Pases por alto* are high passes in which the bull passes below the *muleta* and *pases por bajo* are low passes used to tire the bull.

PASEO. The parade across the ring that precedes a bullfight. The *matadores* lead the *paseo* followed by their teams of *banderilleros* and *picadores*. The *areneros* and other bullring servants including the mule team to drag the carcases of the bulls from the ring bring up the rear.

PASODOBLE. Two Step. Played during the parade across and in most bullrings whilst the *matador* is placing the darts or making a *faena* with the *muleta*. It is an honour for the *matador* to have a *pasodoble* played whilst he is fighting. *Pasodobles* are written and dedicated to popular bullfighters.

PATIO. Courtyard. *Patio de caballos*, see *caballos. Patio de cuadrillas*, the yard leading from the *patio de caballos* to the gate from which the parade starts. It is here that the *matadores* and their *cuadrillas* stand whilst awaiting the signal to make the parade.

PELOTA. Ball. A basque ball game also called Jai-Alai or Fronton.

PETO. The mattress-like padding that is worn by the *picadores'* horses when in the bullring.

PENSION. Boarding-house or family hotel.

PICADOR. The *matador's* mounted assistant. It is the *picador's* job to *picar* the bulls with a lance known as the *pica, puya* or *vara*. The point of the *puya* is pushed into the shoulder muscles of the bull as it charges the horse.

PLAZA DE TOROS. Bullring.

PUNTAZO. A not-too-deep horn wound caused by the *punta* or point of the horn.

QUERENCIA. The place in the bullring where the bull has a preference to be and where he goes on the defensive rather than the attack. Often the bull forms his *querencia* near the gate to the pens or sometimes where he has tossed a man or horse as this action has given him confidence in that particular part of the ring.

QUITE. The taking away of the bull from the horse or a fallen bullfighter.

REJONEADOR. A person who fights and kills the bull entirely from horseback. A totally different art from ordinary bullfighting.

SEGUIDILLA. A type of song of the "deep" *flamenco* class usually associated with the gypsies.

SORTEO. The separating of the bulls on the morning of the fight. The bulls, usually six in number, are paired as far as possible into three equal pairs and the *matadores'* representatives each draw a pair in order of the seniority of the *matador* they represent. The bulls are then separated into individual pens in the order in which they are to be loosed into the ring.

SUERTE. Has many meanings. The most important being luck. The three acts of the bullfight are *suertes*; thus the *suerte de capa, capote, de varas* or *de quites* is the first act, *suerte de banderillas*, the second act and the *suerte de muleta y de matar*, the third and final act.

TALEGUILLA. The skin-tight breeches worn by *matadores* and *banderilleros*. They are made of heavy silk jersey with a gold embroidered satin panel down the outside of each leg.

TASCA. Wine shop. They are similar to the *bistros* of Paris.

TAURINO. Taurine. Pertaining to bullfighting.

TAUROMAQUIA. The art of bullfighting.

TEMPERAMENTO. Temperament.

TIENTA. Testing. The *tientas* are held in the autumn and spring, and while the bullbreeders test and select the cow calves, the bullfighters are given a chance to get into practice for the approaching season.

TIPICO. Typical.

TOREROS. Bullfighters, including *matadores, banderilleros* and *picadores*.

TOROS. Bulls. *Toros Bravos* or *toros de lidia* are the wild bulls bred for use in the bullring.

TRAJE CORTO. The suits worn by bullfighters when fighting at the *tientas* and charity fights. The suit consists of a short bolero jacket and tight trousers and is worn with a tieless white shirt and *sombrero*. It is also known as *traje campero*.

TRAJE DE LUCES. Literally, suit of lights. The suits worn by bullfighters in formal fights. They are so called because of the amount of gold or silver embroidery that they carry. *Matadores* costumes are usually embroidered in gold and those of the *banderilleros* and the jackets of the *picadores* in silver or white beading.

VALIENTES. Brave ones. *Toreros valientes* are brave bullfighters. *Valientes de los asientos* are armchair *toreros*.

VAQUERO. Cowboy. *Vaca* is cow.

VENTA. Sale. The roadside café-bars are also called *ventas*; they correspond to the French *estaminets*.